Progressive Weight Training

Progressive Weight Training

Sport – Fitness – Figure

Eric Taylor

 **SBL** **Springfield Books Limited**

© 1988 Eric Taylor

Published by Springfield Books Limited,
Norman Road, Denby Dale, Huddersfield HD8 8TH,
West Yorkshire, England

First edition 1988

Design: Douglas Martin
Illustrations: John Dillow
Cover illustration: Bryan Ledgard
Typeset in Plantin and
printed and bound in
England by the Alden Press

Photograph credits

The author and publishers are grateful to Nautilus
Sports/Medical Industries, Inc., for kind permission to
reproduce the photographs on pages 38, 39, 40, 41, 42,
43, 44, 45, 46, 47, 48, 49, 50, 51, 52, 53, 54, 55, 56, 57,
58, 59, 60, 61, 62, 63, 65, 66, 67, 68, 69, 70, 72, 73, 74
and 75.
The photograph on page 76 is reproduced by kind
permission of Jack Hickes Photographers Ltd.
All other photographs by KL Photographers, York.

British Library Cataloguing in Publication Data

Taylor, Eric, *1927–*
Progressive weight training.
1. Weight lifting
I. Title
796.4′1   GV546.5

ISBN 0-947655-22-0

Contents

varying degrees of strength and endurance – the value of leg strength – strength for stability – phasing the training programme for sports and athletics – phase one: off-season – phase two: pre-season – phase three: in season – fundamental aims of all training

Progress and motivation in recent years – field events – training for throwing events: throwing the javelin, discus, hammer, putting the shot – suggested routines – training for jumping events – high, long, triple and pole vaulters – track events – how much strength do runners need? – training for different running events – sprinting – middle distance – suggested schedules

Which sport requires the greatest fitness? – basic strengthening routines – more advanced strengthening routines – specific weight training routines for different sports – four basic categories of sports – a word of warning – sports needing particular strength, power and endurance – sports requiring stamina – sports requiring body control and agility – sports requiring hand and eye co-ordination plus stamina – suggested routines for sports in each category

Mental and physical toughness – improved circulatory and respiratory efficiency – endurance training, local and general – circuit training – preparing a circuit – training rate – progression – organisation of circuit training – attraction of circuit training – selecting exercises for circuit training – suggested circuit for 13 to 18-year-olds – circuits for sport – safety considerations – motivation and mental stamina

The psychology of success – the vital ingredient: the will to win – the gymnast who broke her neck and then became a tennis star – the secret of Grand Slam champions – harnessing mental power – attitude – and aggression – and positive thinking – mental rehearsal – programmed for success – confidence and mental approach – the coach – equipment and attention to detail – preparation for the big match – schedule for the day

Acknowledgements

In the writing of this book I have received generous help and encouragement from many people and I should like them all to know that I am deeply grateful. In particular I should like to mention Dennis Kay, who took such care with the photography; Ed Farnham of Nautilus Sports/Medical Industries Inc. for the use of the excellent illustrative material and the Nautilus training philosophy; Mr and Mrs Christie, Stevie Read, Paul Fox, Vicky Nichol of the Viking Hotel gymnasium, and model Jade Campbell, for their help in photographing the exercises. I should also like to record my special thanks to all the sportsmen and sportswomen who, over the years, have kindly let me have their views on weight training. Finally, I should like the lady who typed the entire manuscript, Mrs Ann Milner, to know that I am most appreciative of her efforts on my behalf.

Note on the photographs

Most weight training books are illustrated by photographs of muscular men and women who have been training with weights for years and can lift heavy barbells with comparative ease. This can be misleading for the ordinary man and woman and can cause them to tackle exercises with weights which are too heavy for them.

Consequently, although the illustrations in this book accurately show the positions and movements to be used by all weight trainers, whether advanced or beginners, the weights used by our models are deliberately chosen as those well within the capabilities of beginners.

Chapter One
Why weight training is so popular

Why exactly, is weight training so popular now? The answer may be that everyone can benefit from it; the young and the old, the fit and the injured, the businessman and the beauty queen, the fat and the thin, the athletic and the not so active; all are finding that weight training has much to offer, especially in the way that it caters for individual needs.

Training programmes can be prepared to suit your own particular aim, whether it be general fitness conditioning or tournament toughness. This, of course, is nothing new. For years sportsmen and women have been training with weights to prepare themselves for fierce competition. With ever-rising standards, the need for something more than technical perfection has been recognized – namely strength and stamina, which weight training can provide *par excellence*.

But now, it is not merely for improving performance in sport that weight training is so popular. There is a new wave of enthusiasm from ordinary health-conscious men and women who realise that muscles are meant to be used and that exercising with weights can be a most congenial and effective fitness activity in itself.

Nowhere is this better observed than in the thousands of new gymnasia and leisure centres where, during typical lunchtime and evening sessions, you can find men and women of all ages, pushing and pulling weights of every description. Seminars on fitness and exercise abound in every community, and the results of sports science research are now reaching a mass audience eager to know more about ways to improve their fitness, general health and performance at sport.

A well-informed public no longer confuses weight training with competitive 'body-building' or 'weight-lifting' activities; no longer do people believe the old adage that lifting weights means developing a slow-moving muscle-bound body. No longer do women fear the development of unsightly 'masculine' muscles; quite the reverse. They have found that weight training enhances the feminine form, toning muscles firmly and developing graceful movement. A well-planned schedule of progressive resistance exercises – using free weights or a new machine – can obtain the physical development required more quickly than any other means. It is so effective because it is individually tailored.

There are specific schedules, for use with an appropriate diet, to trim off excess fat, to develop muscular strength and to improve cardio-vascular-respiratory fitness – aerobic fitness. With greater strength comes increased power, a combination of strength and speed, and with greater reserves of stamina comes the ability to sustain a higher standard of skill for longer periods. We all know that tired muscles send out signals of pain and discomfort; the performer's concentration wanes, mistakes are made and a greater conscious effort is needed to carry out movements which at the beginning of play would have been automatic. The resulting nervousness and loss of confidence impair performance. Consequently, a high level of muscular strength and endurance almost invariably produces an improved and more consistent standard of play. This is especially evident when the going gets really tough, as we have often seen on television in long-drawn-out tennis finals and during extra time in football matches.

Obviously, different sports and, indeed, life styles, require different levels and types of fitness and no two individuals are alike in their needs for physical development or rehabilitation, but it is possible to provide a basic guide to training programmes once the activity has been analysed and the individual's strength assessed.

'Fitness' is relative to the task to be tackled; the heavyweight wrestler, for example, needs a different kind of fitness from the squash player or sprinter. Each may be physically fit but each in different physical condition. The same may be said of strength; compare, for example, the explosive power of the shot putter and the enduring effort of the oarsman.

In recognising these different needs, conditioning programmes have become specific and, where needed, more intensive. Weight training has proved itself to be highly effective in this respect, establishing itself as an indispensable part of comprehensive fitness training programmes. In short, more and more people have turned to weight training because it gets results. It contributes to *total* body-fitness, ensuring a balanced development of the whole muscular system – which is something jogging, for instance, could never do. Remarkable progress is evident within days of starting a schedule and though this is not entirely due at first to increased strength and endurance, for some improvement is due to the beginner mastering the technique of lifting the weights, it is nevertheless progress, and progress of any kind is always encouraging. As training continues, increasing both the number of repetitions of an exercise and the weights used, there can be no doubt that the body is responding to the training. 'Nothing succeeds like success': it is a vital incentive for further effort.

This ability to monitor progress accurately means that programmes can be devised to ensure that you always work within safe limits, yet at the same time derive great satisfaction from tangible improvements in physical ability. It also means that there is no need to suffer punishing routines which leave you exhausted immediately afterwards or intolerably stiff the next day. A well-planned routine, bringing steady and sure progress, is the key to successful training. This book aims to give everyone, from the absolute beginner to the top-class competitor, the knowledge to prepare individual training schedules.

In recent years much research has been done into the physiological and psychological effects of exercise generally, and of weight training in particular. A mass of information is now available. Full use has been made of this here, but theoretical discussion has been kept to a minimum. However, in order to help individuals training without the help of a qualified coach, some physiological explanations have been included. So anyone, by following the basic guide-lines, should be able to build a training programme that precisely meets his or her own requirements. Having said this, though, don't underrate the value of a good coach and the support that comes from training with like-minded enthusiasts. There are now many leisure complexes and clubs where weight training can be done with the positive guidance and encouragement of a qualified coach. This motivation is important, for it takes a very determined individual to train continuously with free weights without any moral support. By training in a club you benefit not only from the coaching and social aspects but also from using a much wider range of equipment and specialised machines to add variety to your work-out. This can provide a boost, if interest is flagging. Of course, it all costs money – either in fees or travelling – but to invest in your own fitness is to invest in your future, building a firm basis for a lifetime of good health. And this must be a wise investment.

Finally, remember that weight training is only one of a range of factors which affect fitness. However, the interesting point about weight training is that it generates awareness of all these other factors; it would be absurd to undermine the efforts you have put in at the gym by failing to adopt a sensible attitude to diet, drinking and smoking. Thus, the physical improvement that comes from the progressive resistance exercises with weights reinforces a positive attitude to healthy living. Very quickly the convert to weight training begins to enjoy the exhilaration that comes with it and wakes up in the morning feeling refreshed and full of vitality.

How to start

Before you even think of touching a weight, ask yourself one question: 'Am I fit enough for this kind of exercise?' Give serious thought to any physical disabilities you might have and if in doubt, seek advice from your doctor. Discuss with him your medical history, mention any earlier illnesses or physical weaknesses, genetic or through injury, which might still affect your health. And then, when you are ready to start, remember the advice which every coach would give to the beginner: 'Go easy at first.' Pay no attention to what other people might be doing with weights around you in the gym; they could have been 'pumping iron' for years. That said, you can commence to 'warm up'.

Warming up

Before every training session or sports competition, a thorough warm-up session of six to eight minutes is essential. The aim is twofold; warming and stretching. Exercises should work all the primary muscle groups and joints – neck, shoulders, spine, knee, ankle and toes – through a full range of movement. But a word of warning here; avoid violent stretching or 'bouncing' exercises which use the weight of the head or limbs to increase the range of movement. Such exercises can elongate ligaments and tendons supporting joints and thus do more harm than good. However, the exercise should be vigorous enough to promote a general warmth, make you perspire freely and bring about an increase in the rate and depth of respiration. Much can be done in eight minutes and in addition to the general warming-up routine many weight training coaches recommend a more specific warm-up in which relatively light weights are used as a prelude to the exercises with the heavier ones later, going through the same movements.

'Is all this necessary?' you might ask. Well, there is still a lot we don't know about warming up but research suggests that muscles work more efficiently and there is less risk of injury to muscles and the circulatory system when the body temperature rises above normal. 'If you go from absolute rest to all-out exertion in a few seconds, this could cause failure in circulation to the heart, which might be dangerous if your heart is weak,' writes Laurence Morehouse, Professor of Exercise Physiology at the University of California. There are also psychological benefits to warming up; most weight trainers find they are better prepared for the work-out and get more satisfaction from it if they warm up thoroughly first.

Some suggestions for warming-up routines

Run on the spot or jog around the gym for two or three minutes.

Circle your arms   Stand with your feet astride and swing your arms loosely overhead passing close to your ears, behind the line of your shoulders and forward again. Keep your wrists, elbows and shoulders relaxed the whole time.

Ski swings   With your feet about 15 cm apart, swing your arms loosely and rhythmically backwards and forwards and upwards, at the same time bending and stretching your knees as you would in ski-ing movements.

Kneeling press-ups   Kneel on the floor with your head as close to your knees as you can and your bottom on your heels. Stretch your arms out on the floor in front of your head. Raise your body to the kneeling position so that your shoulders are above your hands. Bend your arms, lowering your chin to the floor. Straighten your arms and return to the starting position.

Lunges   Stand with your feet slightly apart and take a wide step forward with your left leg, bending the knee so that it is immediately above your left foot. Place your left hand on your knee and sink down into the bent position, gradually feeling the muscles of the trailing leg stretching. Repeat with the other leg.

Side bends   Stand with your feet slightly apart, hands by the sides. Bend to your left side, facing front the whole time. Try to reach down your leg a little further each time. Return to start position and repeat to the right.

Lying leg swings   Lie on your left side supporting your head with your left hand, and maintain your body in this position by placing your right hand on the floor in front of your chest. Bring your right knee up to your chest, stretch your leg out in front of your body and then raise it as high as you can away from the floor. Repeat ten times before turning on to your side and doing the same with the left leg.

Neck rotation   Stand with your shoulders loose and drop your head onto your chest. Circle your head slowly over your left shoulder, backwards, upwards and down over the right shoulder. Continue, loosely, slowly and gently. Do not force in any way.

Squat thrusts   This is a much more vigorous exercise. Crouch down with your knees fully bent, hands flat on the floor, a little forward of the feet. Leaning on your hands, jump both legs out backwards then back to the starting position repeatedly.

Trunk rotation   Stand astride, arms stretched out in front, fingers lightly clenched. Keeping the body upright, swing loosely round to the left and then to the right. Allow the arms to swing gently round with the body. Don't bend at the hips.

Stretching

This is the second phase of the warm-up, and it can also be used beneficially at the end of the training session as a means of cooling down and avoiding stiffness. Again, do not force any joints or muscles beyond a comfortable range of movement. Move slowly and deliberately; never bounce or use excessively rhythmic movements of the body to extend the range of movement. Flexibility helps to reduce the risk of injury, so it is worth carrying out a complete stretching routine. You can do the exercises in any order you like. Enjoy them, pick the ones that give you pleasure and then you are less likely to skip them. If you keep to the same routine you can go into it without any conscious thought or decision making. Continue each movement until you sense a slight discomfort of the part of the body being stretched – joint or muscle – and then stop.

Suggestions for stretching exercises

Shoulder girdle stretch   Raise your right arm and reach behind your neck to touch the back of the left shoulder. Lift your left arm and apply a gentle pressure onto the top of the right elbow, pressing it a little further down.

Hurdle stretch   Sit on the floor, right leg stretched forward, left leg tucked as far back as you can, let your body lie slightly backwards supported by the arms.

Quadriceps stretch   Lie on your right side, right arm extended in line with your body, right leg straight. Reach down with your left hand and gently pull your left leg backwards, bending at the knee, to draw your heel up to your seat, stretching the quadriceps of the thigh. Hold in this position for a few seconds, return and then repeat. Change sides and legs.

Back arching   Supporting your body cat-like on hands and feet, legs straight, walk your feet forward as far as you can, arching your back high. Now, keeping your legs and arms straight, lower your hips to the floor, letting your feet slide back so that your back and neck are arched concavely.

Hamstring stretch   You can do this exercise with or without a partner. Sit down with your feet together and legs straight. Your partner sits facing you with legs outstretched and straight, the soles of his feet against yours. Stretch forward and link fingers with your partner. You and your partner take turns to gently pull each other forward as far as you comfortably can. You can do the same exercise on your own with feet against the wall.

Straight leg swinging   Stand with one leg close to a wall and the outside leg bent so that it can be swung easily forwards and backwards. Maintain your balance by resting one hand lightly against the wall.

Knee hugging   Stand on one leg. Raise the other, pulling the knee close to the chest. Change legs.

After your warm-up session you should be feeling ready for training, but remember to listen to what your body is telling you. If you have an ache or pain and don't feel up to a full session, especially if you are not as young as you used to be, then settle for a shorter session. Weight training should be fun, not an ordeal, and designed just for you.

Building your own weight training programme

Not everyone who begins a weight training programme is looking for the same result, so exercises should be selected to cater for your own specific requirements. But beginners should have one common aim – to develop the musculature of the whole body. They can concentrate on specific muscle groups later. So a basic training schedule for beginners should contain at least one exercise for each major muscle group and a power exercise (see Chapter 4). The best exercises to choose would be simple to perform and compatible with a beginner's physical ability.

Below are six basic exercises generally considered suitable:

	Exercise	*Muscle group*
1.	Behind the neck press	Arm and shoulder extensors
2.	Trunk curl	Abdominals
3.	Bench press barbell	Upper arm extensors and chest
4.	Barbell curl	Anterior arm and shoulder flexors
5.	Bent forward rowing	Arm and dorsal
6.	Squat	Power

The exercises are arranged in order so that muscle groups have adequate recovery time before being exercised again.

How much weight should you handle?

One of the greatest temptations facing you as a weight trainer is that of adding an extra disc of weight before you are quite ready. There is no need to try for maximum poundage. Keep to the main principle of *progressive* resistance and avoid jumping up the weight too quickly; it can be dangerous and disheartening.

The weight you start with will depend upon your build, age and present state of fitness but it is easy to decide just how much weight to use with the exercises. Try them first with light weights, and if that is too easy then add more until only about between six and ten repetitions can be managed comfortably, without jerking the bar or gasping for breath. Once you can do more than a dozen repetitions easily with the new weight then it is time to add weight. But do take it steadily. There are no short cuts to physical development. Push yourself gradually and safely. Take care especially if you are working alone that you don't get stuck with a weight that you don't know how to get rid of safely. For the first few sessions some coaches recommend working with a light weight for a high number of repetitions. Later, you may find that three sets of six repetitions of the basic exercises will produce greater gains in strength. After you have determined the starting weights then enter them on a record chart (see page 23). You can then see at a glance the progress you are making as the chart is completed at regular intervals during the course of training.

Training sessions – length and frequency

Most weight trainers agree that a three-training-days-a-week programme produces the best results. This applies to beginners and experts alike. The reason for this is that muscles have an optimum rate of development and beyond a certain point it cannot be speeded up. When muscles are worked maximally for a short period of time they require time to recover and adapt themselves to the new work-load before they can be effectively exercised again, both in the training session and also in between the sessions. During the training session this recovery can take place whilst other muscle groups are being exercised so the session can continue without rest periods between lifts. A day's rest between sessions would suffice, but when planning your weekly programme it might be simpler to fix training days for the same day and time every week, say Monday, Wednesday and Friday, with Saturday and Sunday off.

For most purposes a schedule taking approximately thirty minutes would produce good results, but many coaches believe that an ideal programme would take about an hour. However, we do not live in an ideal world, so we have to ensure that we get the most out of the time we can afford. The shorter the session the more important it is to use it effectively, so we will look next at the equipment to be used and the training methods.

Chapter Two
Training methods and equipment

In spite of the vast amount of research that has taken place in the field of exercise physiology during the last twenty years, there is still no real agreement about which is the most effective method of training with weights.

Perhaps the divergence of opinion on methods arises from this: there are so many factors which affect success that it is difficult to evaluate the importance of each one. Training records clearly show the time spent, poundage and repetitions used in a weight training schedule, but we have no means of measuring the determination and enthusiasm of the weight trainer. No-one can accurately estimate the effect of this motivating force which drives you out to the gymnasium on dark, wet, blustery winter nights and makes you persevere despite the demands of studies, career, or a family. One thing though is sure: whatever the training method, success will follow only when the willpower is there and harnessed to the method best suited to your own circumstances. In the end it is for you to choose from the recognised methods available.

Basic methods or systems of weight training

There are many ways of applying progressive resistance with weights to a muscle group; you can have a high number of lifts or repetitions (reps) with a low weight, or a small number with heavy weights, or one of the permutations in between, depending on whether you want to concentrate upon developing cardio-vascular fitness and muscular endurance or strength and explosive power. But here again you cannot be too categorical; the amount of weight needed to stimulate muscular development is a very individual matter. Broadly speaking, however, a high number of repetitions with a light weight tends to develop muscular endurance and few repetitions with a very heavy weight develop strength, power, and bulk. For cardio-vascular fitness the heart rate needs to be kept at a high level for between fifteen and thirty minutes. Some of the main weight training methods are given below.

The three sets method

This method is useful for beginners and individuals working with only one set of weights. By doing three sets, one after the other, there is no need to adjust the weights until the next exercise is begun; this saves time.

The number of repetitions depends upon whether you are aiming for strength or stamina. A poundage heavy enough to keep the maximum possible repetitions below ten is normally used for strength development, and a lighter poundage, allowing thirty or more rapid repetitions, for stamina (but see also Chapter 8).

Many coaches stress the importance of relaxing muscles in between each bout of exercise, in order to give the circulatory system a chance to eliminate the waste products of fatigue and speed recovery, but this relaxation period need be no longer than about a minute plus the time taken to adjust the weight for the next exercise. Shake your arms and legs loosely whilst taking a few deep breaths. However, if the rest period between each bout of exercise is too long, say about four or five minutes, then the cardio-vascular system will benefit less from the training session than if the heart rate were kept to a higher level for a longer period through having no longer than about a minute's rest between sets and exercises. No two individuals are alike, though, and it is better to err on the side of safety – progressing gradually and avoiding over-exertion, particularly in the third set. You should not continue with repetitions of an exercise once the movements have become jerky and uneven.

When you can perform three sets of ten repetitions of an exercise then you can increase the poundage, thus increasing the resistance to the muscle groups involved, then progress into a new phase of training. In this way improvements in strength and cardio-vascular efficiency can be made without increasing the duration of the training session.

The sequence method

In the sequence method you do a full set of ten repetitions before passing on to the next exercise station. In this way you can go with hardly a pause from one set of an exercise to the next until the whole sequence is finished, and then begin the whole sequence again. This method is only possible in gymnasia where there is ample weight training equipment available so that you do not have to spend time adjusting the weight or resistance.

The training task is usually that of three sequences or circuits. As with the three sets method, the weight recommended for each exercise is one allowing no more than ten repetitions. At the end of two weeks of this type of training, test yourself on each exercise to see how many repetitions you can now do. If there is a marked increase beyond ten, add to the poundage until you can just do ten.

Naturally, when many people are training together it will not always be possible to alter the weight on a bar but there can sometimes be a heavy routine or a light one from which to choose. Progress can also be made by gradually trying to cut down the time taken for each sequence or circuit.

The sequence method of weight training is also useful for developing cardio-vascular efficiency, for the activity raises the heart rate to a high level and keeps it there for the duration of the session. As with the three sets method, though, take care to avoid making excessive demands upon your physical ability; at the end of a session you should not be left with a feeling of nausea or complete exhaustion.

With sequence training, as with all the many variables in weight training methods, *you* decide whether the emphasis in the training programme should be on cardio-vascular fitness and muscular endurance or on strength development. Broad guide-lines for the preparation of sequence training schedules are set out below.

For cardio-vascular endurance with the sequence method

o   Pass directly from finishing one exercise to the next one with minimal delay
o   Use less weight with high repetitions at each exercise station
o   Complete more sequences than the basic three
o   Take shorter recuperative periods in between each sequence

For developing strength with the sequence method

o   Allow at least a minute's interval between finishing one exercise and starting the next
o   Use heavier weights allowing perhaps only six or eight repetitions
o   Tackle fewer but more strenuous sequences or circuits
o   Pause to lower the respiratory and heart rates between each sequence

The sequence or circuit method of weight training can be a most effective way of getting many people through a routine in a short time. There is no need for everyone to start at the first exercise; a start can be made at any station provided the trainee continues around the circuit in the order in which it is set out. If there are ten duplicated pieces of weight training equipment then ten pairs of weight trainees can start together, moving on to the next piece at a given signal. Using this system it is advisable to have the option of a heavy or light routine at each station. As a guide to the choice of weight to use with the exercise, the final repetition in each set should be difficult to perform.

The sequence method is effective but it should not be the only one you consider. Individuals progress in different ways and at different rates; your muscles may respond readily to a higher sets and repetitions routine with only a short recuperative period in between each, whilst your training partner's muscles might improve by another method altogether. There is always room for experimentation along recognised guide-lines. Chart your progress carefully and, by trial and error, select the methods that suit you best. It is here that the advice of a coach can be most helpful, especially when it comes to advanced training methods.

Progression and advanced training methods

Your progress will at first be remarkable. But then you have to face the fact that progression can be spasmodic, unpredictably variable or, even worse, completely elusive! All these states are normal, but you need not feel powerless when experiencing them. Try one of the following approaches:

○ Increasing the number of repetitions in each set
○ Increasing repetitions daily and weight weekly
○ Increasing the number of sets
○ Increasing the weight with sets of diminishing repetitions
○ Using a heavy and light routine

By the time you need to introduce variety into your routine you will already have amassed a good deal of personal experience and have got to know your body better, so you will be able to make choices according to your aims and capabilities. Some further explanations on these alternatives to the basic training programme are given below.

Increasing the number of repetitions in each set

A safe but effective way of making progress is by increasing the number of repetitions in each set weekly but trying to complete the whole schedule in the same amount of time. The effect of speeding up the movements causes your muscles to check momentum and change direction of movement, which increases the overload. The important principle on all progressive resistance training is to exercise muscles as thoroughly as possible by working them intensely within a short period of time.

Increasing repetitions daily and weight weekly

One significant advantage of this double progression is that daily progress is possible as well as weekly (if you train every day). On the first training day you complete a schedule as planned and then on successive days gradually increase the repetitions in each set. The ability to increase the number of repetitions indicates a corresponding increase in strength. In the early stages of training more repetitions might be possible because of improvements in your technique – getting the 'knack' of the exercise.

By the end of the week an individual in daily training who could initially do only seven arm curls in three sets, might have progressed to three sets of ten repetitions. This is the time for more weight to be added to reduce the repetitions. This two-pronged progression is an ideal way of developing stamina as well as strength.

Increasing the number of sets

Weight trainers using this method handle the same poundages for the exercises throughout the week but as each day passes they try to build up an extra set. For example, on day two they might do three sets of ten squats and a fourth set of two. Gradually this fourth set can be increased to ten and the weight would then be increased. This more severe type of training should only be undertaken by those who are already physically very strong and then only if there is a particular need for extra strength.

Increasing the weight with sets of diminishing repetitions (the pyramid system)

This method is definitely only for advanced weight training schedules. The target with the diminishing repetitions routine is to work up to one supreme lift of the heaviest weight possible for the exercise. Advanced weight trainers start with a weight that can be lifted four or five times, then for the second set more weight is added which perhaps permits only two repetitions, and finally yet more weight is added so that the exercise can only be done once. The object of the diminishing repetitions method is maximal contraction for the final movement. If the additional weight for the third set has not been judged accurately, more weight can be added for a single lift.

Sometimes this method is called the 'pyramid' system; a variation is to work towards a final lift as described above and then to 'taper off' by reducing the weight so that five or six repetitions can be done, rather than stopping suddenly after the maximal effort.

'Pyramid' training is not a regular form of training but a means of bringing variety into a training programme that appears to have reached a plateau as far as progress is concerned. It could head you towards further progress. But so also could patience.

There is a reverse pyramid system in which the repetitions decrease as the weight increases and then on reaching a single lift the repetitions increase as the weight decreases.

Two other systems deserve a mention: the cyclic method and the split routine.

The cyclic method

This is a variation of the three sets method. During the first three weeks the beginner does the usual three sets of ten repetitions, then in weeks four to eight, three sets of five repetitions (using heavier weights which will allow no more than five repetitions) and then in weeks eight to twelve, three sets of three repetitions. Trainees using this variation produce significantly greater gains in strength and power than those who train over a similar period using three sets of six repetitions the whole time. Clearly the use of few repetitions with heavier weights taxes the muscle groups more severely and causes them to respond or adapt more positively.

The split routine

With this routine the exercises are divided between alternate days so that one day certain groups are exercised and on the next day, the other group. Thus, on Wednesdays you could work on six exercises which concentrate primarily upon the arm, chest and abdominals and on the next training day, say Friday, exercises for the back, leg and hip muscles. If you don't have time for a long work-out you may find this a useful way of making progress: I have seen it work successfully in lunch-hour sessions, for example.

A possible split routine could be:

Routine A	Routine B
Bench press	Bent over rowing
Barbell curls	The back squat
Trunk curls	Trunk raising backwards with weight
Lateral dumb-bell raise	Torso Arm machine pull
Double bent arm pullover	Leg lunge
Overhead press	Chinning behind neck

When working a split routine take care to keep a diary of your work-outs. You cannot always be sure of your memory to tell you which routine you are on that day.

How much progress?

Progress in the early stages of weight training progress is always rapid as a result of three factors. First of all there is 'motor learning'; you get the feeling of the movement and can do it with less effort. Then there is an improvement in nervous co-ordination so that more muscle fibres can be contracted by the same nervous stimulus. And finally, the exercise produces muscular development.

This dramatic progress delights the weight trainer during the early weeks. As training proceeds, however, progress becomes increasingly difficult to achieve. It is at this point that you must ask yourself: 'How strong do I want to be?' There is little point in going willy-nilly after greater and greater strength, for after you have reached a certain level not only is progress more difficult but also you have to spend a disproportionate amount of time to achieve small gains.

WEIGHT TRAINING PROGRESS CHART

Name _____   Weight: _____
                                                begun: _____

Exercise	Classification or muscle group	Date: Weeks:			Date: Weeks:		
		Weight	Reps	Sets	Weight	Reps	Sets
1.							
2.							
3.							
4.							
5.							
6.							
Additional exercises							
7.							
8.							
9.							
10.							

NOTES: (Variations in sets/reps, modifications to programme, and
       effects observed)

Training equipment – free weights or machines?

The catalogues of weight training equipment can confuse the beginner wishing to buy equipment for use at home, for there is a wide variety available, some of which is very expensive. However, you may find it convenient to train at home; it saves time and money in travelling and membership fees, and a home gym could give you greater flexibility about when and for how long you train. Naturally you will not have all the equipment to be found in a well-equipped fitness centre but you can gather enough together to cater for your physical development, especially in the early stages.

Seek advice from a reputable sports outfitter and other weight trainers before making your final choice of equipment. Some bars, for example, begin to bend when more than 200 pounds are added; plastic coated weights can take up a lot of space on a bar, thereby limiting the load. Be sure to buy enough weights to cope with the heaviest exercises and have plenty of small ones so that you can progressively increase the resistance at two or three pounds a time. Many weights now come in metric measurements. A simple approximate way of working out the poundage is to multiply by two and add 10 per cent. Thus 20 kg equals $20 \times 2 = 40$ plus $10\% = 44$ pounds, approximately.

Minimum equipment for a home gym
1 barbell, length 150 cm or 5 ft
1 barbell sleeve
4 barbell locking collars
2 dumb-bell rods, length 30 cm or 1 ft
2 dumb-bell locking collars
Disc weights totalling 75 kg (about 160 pounds)

For example:
  6 discs at $2\frac{1}{2}$ kg
  6 discs at 5 kg
  4 discs at $7\frac{1}{2}$ kg
  Total . . . 75 kg or ($75 \times 2 - 150$ plus $10\% = 165$ pounds approx.)

You will see from Chapter 4 that some exercises are done on a bench. A wooden one could be most uncomfortable once heavy weights are used and you really need one that can be adjusted to incline for variations of exercises. Specially designed benches usually have additional features such as barbell supports and padded bars for special leg exercises. If the cost is prohibitive then advertise for a used one in the specialist magazines and look in their classified columns of equipment for sale. You should have no difficulty in finding what you need. Additional equipment can be bought later if required and if you still wish to train at home; but you may wish to consider an alternative to training with free weights – the exercise machine.

During the last twenty years, the increasing popularity of weight training in well-equipped gyms has meant that facilities now exist in most areas for exercise employing progressive resistance on machines which can provide more efficient methods of developing strength and general fitness. What do we mean by efficient? Simply achieving maximum returns from a given amount of time and effort. These machines allow you to apply resistance progressively, precisely and safely. Less time is lost in adjusting weights and there is not the same need to have 'spotters' standing by to help when very heavy weights are used (see 'Hazards and safety precautions', later in this chapter). The weight resistance from a machine can be adjusted simply by changing the position of a locking pin; for this reason alone, more people can exercise in the gym in a shorter time than if they were all using free weights. Machines are space saving, convenient and often more fun to use.

Naturally, free weights and exercise machines have their respective merits, although they both depend for their results upon the quality of the overload or resistance applied to the muscles being exercised. But the barbell is limited by gravity; it acts in a straight line up and down, whereas most body movements are rotary in nature. You can quickly see, for example, how the resistance of gravity varies if you think of the arm curl exercise (pages 45–6). When a barbell is used for this movement of bringing the fist up to the shoulder, gravity imposes maximum resistance only in the approach to mid-point of the exercise, it is not exerted against the muscle at a constant pressure throughout the range of movement. Machines redirect gravity, employing a rotary resistance to provide muscles with overload throughout the full range of movement. The machines are also designed to provide variable resistance in exact proportion to the needs of each movement, for muscles are more mechanically efficient in some positions than in others. A specially designed cam can give the exercised muscle a mechanical advantage at its weakest range of movement and a corresponding mechanical advantage where it is more powerful. Think again of the arm curl; the most difficult part is the first movement, and it becomes easier as the elbow flexors shorten and the weight approaches the shoulder. A machine can, at this point, put more resistance against the working muscle group and thus develop strength in this range too. However, movement with a machine is at a constant speed, whereas most of the movements in sport and everyday activities involve considerable accelerations or changes of speed. Free weights cater well for the development of speed and acceleration; thus, dumb-bell and barbell exercises can complement the benefits to be gained from machines.

Another advantage of using exercise machines is in achieving specificity of training and development. We know from research into motor learning that the most efficient way of increasing skill proficiency is to practise the skill in question exactly in the way it is to be performed. Similarly, to develop strength in the muscles used for a particular movement, we should concentrate on providing resistance to those muscle structures directly contributing to this activity. Then you can apply the increased power gained from this specific strengthening routine to the desired skill. However, there is no physiological basis for believing that we can improve performance by practising the skills of a sport against a *heavier* resistance than would be met in the course of the game. To use a heavier bat, club, racquet, or football in the skill training for the game, can do more harm than good by disturbing the natural pattern of motor responses. To add an artificial resistance to a movement can cause confusion of these motor responses and thus a direction of the desired skill. It cannot be over-emphasised: skill training must *not* involve overload.

Specific exercises must be employed to strengthen the muscles used in a particular movement and when that movement is of a rotary nature then machines can be most beneficial. However, there are valid arguments in favour of the use of free weights. It is often said that these exercises develop many muscle groups other than the prime movers involved; when the barbells are used to give dynamic exercise to one particular muscle group many other groups have to work hard to maintain body balance and the stability necessary for the prime movers to work at all (see Chapter 3). This physical capacity for balancing opposing muscle groups and maintaining body balance needs developing for improved co-ordination and utilisation of muscle power in everyday life and sport. It is also argued that since the machines do the work of balancing and stabilising the body they fail to develop the other groups of muscles in the same way that free weight training does. On the other hand, whilst it is true that barbell exercises do develop this element of balance, it is only required by those who are lifting weights competitively and has little carry-over value for other sports and activities. Free weight training with barbells and dumb-bells gives you a greater range of exercises, thus adding variety to your training schedule.

What, then, should you do? Which training method should you follow? Ideally you should try to get the best from both worlds; machines and free weights each have their advantages and drawbacks but they can complement each other. Consider your own particular circumstances, the proximity of gyms, the availability of free weights and the expense. Then do the best you can to make progress effectively and safely.

Hazards and safety precautions

Weight training is one of the safest of all physical fitness activities. It is dangerous only when carelessness, horseplay and foolhardiness take the place of common-sense codes of practice. (See also 'Safety considerations in circuit training', Chapter 8.)

Hernia

What about hernia, or rupture, as it is commonly called? Interabdominal pressure is raised during an all-out lift and it is true that if there are any inherent weaknesses in the abdominal muscular walls then severe weight training will find them out. The weakness is not necessarily caused by the weight training, it merely brings it to light. Sooner or later the herniation would probably have occurred anyway, in an everyday act like lifting a heavy piece of furniture or machinery.

Muscle strain

It would be difficult for even the most enthusiastic of weight trainers to tear a muscle through lifting progressively heavier weights in the normal resistance routines because tension within the muscle groups develops too slowly to cause such an injury. Strains of ligaments and tendons as well as injuries to joints are sometimes caused when the progression to heavier weights is made too swiftly; you may lose your balance during an unduly heavy exercise and, in trying to prevent weights from crashing to the floor, an abnormally heavy strain might be thrown upon a muscle group not intended to carry such loads. This is one reason why, in advanced training with free weights, a 'spotter' or training partner should be ready to assist with the correct positioning of the weights at the beginning and end of each exercise.

Slipped disc

Another bogy often raised is that of the 'slipped disc', and it is true that disc lesions are often caused through lifting a heavy object when the back is rounded and perhaps leaning forward in the stretching position. Mothers leaning forward over the pram handle to lift the baby out are sometimes caught with the excruciating pain that indicates damage has been done. Stretching over furniture and pushing forcibly upwards is another common cause. But the injury is really brought about by adopting a faulty position, not exerting a strong force in lifting or pushing. The maxim for weight lifting is 'a firm base and a straight back'; don't bend downwards with a rounded back and jerk up heavy weights. If you do, something will have to give, and invariably it will be the small muscles that keep the disc in position between the vertebrae. The disc is then liable to pop out and press on the nerve roots serving the lumbar region, the buttock, and down the back of the thigh. Pain will run down the back and leg in these areas.

When lifting the weight from the floor adopt a position with your feet close to the bar and on the same line, lower your hips, bend your knees and keep your head up with your back straight. Remember, you lift the weight with your legs and not with your back muscles. Master the technique of each lift with a light weight before attempting a maximum lift.

Heart strain

Does weight training throw too much of a strain on the heart? It can be dangerous if the wrong technique is used and if you are already suffering from heart trouble. If you hold your breath whilst attempting a heavy lift then the pressure inside the chest cavity increases tremendously. Blood is forced out of the pulmonary vascular bed into the arteries together with the blood pumped from the heart. This increases the outward flow and blood pressure in the arteries rises. At the same time, owing to the abnormally high compression within the chest cavity, the blood from the veins in unable to force its way back to the heart. The heart is unable to maintain a steady supply to the arteries and the blood pressure drops alarmingly – so much so that the pulse beat may disappear altogether. Straining to lift the weight compresses the heart and the volume of the compartment for the returning venous blood is greatly reduced. If, when the lift is completed, the breath is released explosively, the heart immediately dilates and there is an enormous rush of blood into its chambers. The extra flow causes the arterial pressure to rise dramatically again. These sudden changes are dangerous and it is obvious that you should not undertake strenuous weight training if you have any circulatory or respiratory weaknesses; in any case, you should never strain to such an extent that you are forced to hold your breath.

The advice given by most coaches is simple: breathe in before you start and out as you make the effort. You might find this hard to do at first as it goes against your natural inclination, but you will soon get used to doing it that way every time. You will also find that many weight trainers exaggerate the breathing so that it can be clearly heard; breathing in through the nose deeply and exhaling forcibly through the mouth. Never hold your breath.

Safety code

To sum up, there is an element of risk in weight training, but if your training progresses gradually in poundage and repetitions and you follow the safety code given below there is no need to fear any harmful effects.

1. Always warm up and stretch muscles and joints first.
2. Progress gradually in poundage and repetitions.
3. Remember the maxim: 'firm base, straight back'.
4. If in doubt, see your doctor before starting a programme.
5. Make sure all equipment is properly adjusted.
6. Remember to breathe freely in the way described above.
7. Do all movements with a steady rhythm, not laboured or jerkily.
8. Stop immediately if training causes nausea or excessive breathlessness.

Chapter Three
Successful weight training for men and women

Weight training is far more successful when you know exactly what you are doing and why. And certainly everyone wants to get the most from time spent exercising.

With weights you are working your muscles against a gradually increased resistance, so let us have a look at how muscles are constructed and how they react to this work. Then we shall know better how to get the most from each training session.

Muscle action

Muscles consist of bundles of long tough fibres and whenever you lift anything, some of them are brought into action. Take up a pen and only a few fibres of the arm flexor muscles contract; pick up a heavy case and place it on the table and many more bundles of fibres need to work. The brain sends messages to the muscles to activate the fibres. If in the course of a normal day you are never required to move anything heavy, then, naturally, the brain never activates more than the few muscle fibres that are needed. Consequently, the muscles of people in sedentary jobs are rarely fully stimulated and they remain small and weak, simply through lack of use. Remember the warning given by the Post Office about the sub-post office: 'Use it or lose it'.

When you begin to train with weights you start to use much more of your physical potential; a greater proportion of muscle fibres are brought into action and remarkably pleasing changes become evident: your body begins to alter its shape, you feel more energetic, and look more lively.

What is happening?

If a heavy weight is lifted repeatedly, the load is shunted from one set of fibres to another, so that those which have become fatigued have time to rest and recover. The heavier the weight, the greater the proportion of muscle fibres involved and therefore the fewer that are left to relieve those which are fatigued. Consequently, after a few repetitions with a heavy weight, the working muscles become thoroughly fatigued and incapable of further effort until they have been rested long enough to recover. And in the process of recovering they develop to cope with the new work load.

So muscular strength can be developed by exercising muscles against a gradually increased resistance; this is known as the 'principle of overload' or 'progressive resistance'. Some exercises lend themselves more than others to the application of overload because the movements can be done in exactly the same manner each time and the load is easily adjusted to increase the resistance. Weight training with free weights or machines is therefore one of the most effective ways of developing muscular strength and endurance.

When heavy work is done at regular training sessions and the weight gradually increased, narrow muscle fibres become broader and stronger. Fewer fibres can then do the work previously done by more. The development of these narrow fibres is usually described as 'hypertrophy' – a natural and beneficial development, whether it be of skeletal muscles or those of the heart.

Group action of muscles

For well co-ordinated movements, many groups of muscles have to work together as a team. One group (the prime movers) cause the action, another group (the synergists, or neutralisers) works statically to prevent unnecessary movements in other parts of the body, another group (the fixators or stabilisers) will fix the base from which the prime movers work and yet another group (the antagonists) will relax, paying out the slack in a controlled manner, to ensure a smooth movement of the working joint. The importance of aiming for a balanced development of the muscular system is obvious, and you have to take this into consideration when devising your own training schedules for specific aims.

Specific effects

Training is always more effective when the aim is clear and the programme well planned. Weight training carried out in a haphazard and irregular way never brings satisfactory returns for your efforts.

Think carefully about the effects you want from your training; it can give you strength, power, endurance, cardio-vascular fitness and a tremendous boost to your self-confidence which, in turn, can allow you to make maximal use of all your physical attributes. Once you have decided upon the bias of your training schedule and selected your exercises, work out your timetable carefully so that other commitments do not distract you from your programme. Now you can apply yourself conscientiously to a routine that you know is based on sound principles and is sure to succeed in achieving its aims.

Strength

Most coaches agree that although no two individuals respond in exactly the same way to progressive resistance exercise, it can be said generally that the development of strength depends upon:

1. The demands made upon the muscle (the degree of overload).
2. The duration of the demands.
3. The regularity and frequency of those demands.

Very few sports or physical activities by themselves make enough demands of the muscular system and therefore some other form of training is needed if strength is to be improved.

It is not possible to be absolutely categorical about how such gains in strength are best achieved with weight training because it has always been difficult to measure and compare different groups of people following different training schedules. To select two identical groups of people, with identical proportions of muscle and fat in different body types, would be well nigh impossible, and to ensure that one group followed a particular programme and the other group another with equal zeal would also be asking the impossible. So, we cannot yet back advice with valid test results. But we can give the considered opinion of experienced coaches who have been training athletes over many years, and this is that muscular strength, power, and size increase most quickly when heavy weights permitting only a few repetitions are used. The number of repetitions varies usually between six and three.

Speed and acceleration

Success in many sports depends upon the speed at which the skills can be performed. But no matter how many games of football, tennis or baseball you play, after a certain point, no further gains of speed are going to be made merely by playing the game.

Whether weight training can improve speed and acceleration or not is a hotly debated topic. There is no conclusive evidence available from tests. But here again, the opinion of coaches and the experience of top class players (see Chapters 5, 6 and 7) seem to indicate that weight training can be beneficial for those needing that extra bit of zip off the mark. Rapid lifting with lighter weights is recommended for developing speed and acceleration.

Power

Power is a product of strength and speed. It can be developed by using exercises which call for an explosive effort from several groups together, and this must be an essential part of weight training for athletics and sport. Power training will include:

1. Combination exercises closely imitating powerful movements required in the activity.
2. Sets of exercises in which the weight is moved through its full range as quickly as possible.
3. Rapid movements to full extent with lighter weights. (See Chapters 6 and 7 for details.)

At the top level of competition, power can be as important as skill, so weight training for power can contribute almost as much to success as can practice of skills.

Flexibility

There is still the occasional doubting Thomas who believes that weight training adversely affects flexibility and agility. There is no physiological reason why it should, if a well-balanced weight training schedule is practised. On the contrary, reports of studies into the effects of weight training suggest that those who train regularly are often more flexible generally than those who simply play sports. Carry out all exercises through the full range of movement after you have completed a thorough warm-up and stretching routine.

Cardio-vascular fitness

Weight training exercises can form a valuable base for aerobic circuit training where the heart rate is lifted to a higher level for a period of time which would vary according to the age and physical condition of the individual.

Once again, the particular value of using weights to sustain the aerobic element of a work-out is that you are sure to be exercising, in a balanced way, all the muscles of the body, some of which you would not often use in everyday life (see Chapter 8).

Women and weights

Ever since women first competed in the Olympic Games half a century ago there have been heated arguments about the effects of vigorous exercise on women. Specialists in physical education declared that women should not copy men in their sports but should devise and develop sports more suitable to the frailer frame of women. But no real evidence was ever produced in support of their argument, and now women are wielding weights and tackling training schedules that would have shocked Olympic athletes a couple of decades ago. Few people would argue with the words of the Queen's surgeon, Sir Arthur Porritt, that 'structurally it has been amply proved that a woman's frame is just as adequate as a man's.'

There is, however, a difference in the way that a woman's body responds to weight training. Whilst gains in muscular strength, tone and flexibility are undoubtedly made, there is not the same development of muscular mass as with a man following a similar training programme. Consequently there is no reason for women to fear developing a physique like an Amazonian shot-putter. In fact the reverse is more likely to happen; weight training combined with a suitable diet can give a woman a trim graceful figure and reshape the body in the way that she wants. Anyone who has seen what can happen to the female figure after a crash diet without accompanying body building exercises would agree that what is left can be far less attractive – the bare bones and wasted muscle of an angular frame. The muscles make the curves. They can mould the shoulders to balance the breadth of hips, flatten the abdomen to give greater definition to the waist, tighten up the gluteals of the buttocks to give a sleeker silhouette and strengthen pectoral muscles to give extra support to the breasts.

But muscular development is only part of the story. Exercise is the flywheel that sets in motion all the body's other systems – digestive, nervous, endocrine, reproductive, circulatory and respiratory – making them more efficient. Improved well-being is seen in the attractive glow of physical fitness and the lively manner of those with energy to spare. Seldom do these women seem fatigued.

What is this phenomenon of fatigue? It is brought on by a combination of factors, psychological as well as physical. There is the fatigue that comes from vigorous muscular activity producing oxygen debt and the waste products of physiological fatigue which have to be dispersed; and there is also also the fatigue brought on by the mental conditions of frustration, boredom, stress and anxiety. These causes of stress can be relieved by systematic exercise with weights; strange though it may seem, exercise can actually generate fresh energy. Women are finding that after a session in the gym at the end of a working day, they leave feeling much livelier than when they went in.

One beneficial side effect of weight training is the way it develops self-confidence – in the business of everyday life or in athletic competition. Somehow it releases the ability for you to develop your optimum potential. The remarkable progress that has been made in women's athletics and sports performance in recent years surely has proved what can be done. Naturally it has called for a high degree of dedication and self-discipline. To succeed now in world class competition, it is not enough to have a natural aptitude for sport and highly developed technical skill. You must also train for strength and stamina to use your technique to maximum effect under the severe stress of competition. It is tough at the top; Martina Navratilova and Chris Evert Lloyd are examples of world class players who have benefited from taking up weight training.

It all takes time. But not such a lot. For the woman who wants to feel fitter, be more energetic and improve her figure, half an hour of weight training, three times a week, would suffice. And really there is nothing new or revolutionary in this;

girls in American and British schools were training with weights and Indian clubs in the late nineteenth century, and over a hundred years ago Empress Elizabeth of Austria had a daily work-out with weights in her palace gym to preserve her wasp waist!

Types of exercise for women

Nearly all weight training exercises are suitable for women, provided that adjustments are made to poundage and repetitions according to each individual's ability. Movement by movement, there is little difference between a man's performance and that of a woman in the same athletic event. The mechanics of the muscle action in putting the shot, for example, are the same for a man as for a woman. It seems sensible then for women to employ the same training methods.

Frequently, with both women and men, inadequate strength and insufficient endurance are the fundamental causes of poor style, particularly towards the end of a match or event, and training time is often wasted in practising a technique which the muscles are not strong enough to perform correctly. This is where a good coach can help; he, or she, can best decide how the time available for training can be divided between the six basic attributes of good performance: strength, stamina, skill, speed, agility and motivation. (See also Chapter 7.)

Menstruation and pregnancy

Some women tend to take things easy during menstruation, but research has shown that there is no physiological reason for doing so. Naturally, there is bound to be a good deal of variation from one individual to the next, but fit, active women usually find that exercise is a help; it relieves stress and has a beneficial effect upon pre-menstrual tension. There is no evidence to support the argument that rigorous exercise reduces fertility.

Weight training during pregnancy is a matter for more caution. Although many experienced weight trainers have continued to follow a modified weight training programme during pregnancy, it would be safer to seek medical advice first. Certainly no-one should begin weight training when pregnant.

During the post-natal period, care should be taken not to stretch weakened muscles through physical exercise. Resume weight training gradually; a six months' lapse is often recommended. Callisthenics and swimming can be used as a gentle re-introduction to more intensive schedules of weight training, which will speed complete recovery by strengthening abdominals and back muscles and generally improve posture.

Weight training in the middle years

There is no age at which you suddenly cease to be young, but there is no doubt that most people regard forty as a definite landmark. There are, of course, seemingly ageless forty-plus people who appear younger than their chronological years and indeed, physiologically, may be younger than thirty-year-olds, but, as a general rule when you reach forty you should start thinking a little more carefully about exercise. It is the time for systematic conditioning rather than the sporadic bursts of violent activity provided by badminton or squash. Not one person in a thousand would stop in the middle of a game because of feeling over-tired, that enough was enough. But weight training can be planned to give just enough exercise and no more.

It is gradual, progressive and safe because there is no-one to beat. It is geared to each individual's ability. And it is never too late to start weight training, although the older you are the more gradual must be the introductory phase. Anyone who has been physically inactive for several years should not suddenly begin heaving weights and sweating profusely in the gym. Muscles which have been used to a more easy-going existence will react adversely to this sudden harsh treatment.

It would be wise to spend a week or two on general mobilising and stretching exercises so that joints and muscles get used to working through their full range of movement before having additional resistance put upon them. Then, following the principles set out in Chapter 3, a schedule or progressive weight training exercises can be built up using light weights. Avoid the temptation of adding heavy weights too soon: progress will be made more surely in this way. Overdoing it, particularly after the forty mark has been passed, can cause excessive tiredness and thereby increase susceptibility to illness. Somehow one has to strike a balance between moderate beneficial exercise and hanging up your trainers and racquets for good. There should be no sudden change in mid-life from being actively sporting to being the sedentary spectator. Naturally, the vigorous, body contact games will gradually be dropped but there are plenty of other beneficial physical recreations that can take their place; swimming, cycling, walking, are ideal activities to complement a weight training routine.

Remember, it is a safe, progressive exercise that is needed by both men and women in their middle years and a carefully drawn up weight training routine can satisfy this need and help you to enjoy the best years of your life.

Chapter Four

Basic weight training exercises with free weights and machines

The weight training exercises described in this chapter have been selected to satisfy the basic requirements for building your own programme. There are literally hundreds of weight training exercises; those described here have been selected because they employ most effectively the principles of progressive weight training.

These basic exercises have been classified anatomically according to the major muscle groups involved. Power exercises, where several muscle groups work together, have been given a special classification. (These are referred to in some publications as 'total body exercises'.) The six major groups are as follows.

1. Power or 'total body' exercises
2. Arm and shoulder exercises
3. Abdominal exercises
4. Leg exercises
5. Dorsal or back exercises
6. Chest exercises

Muscles of trunk and shoulder girdle from the front

Muscles of trunk and shoulder girdle from behind

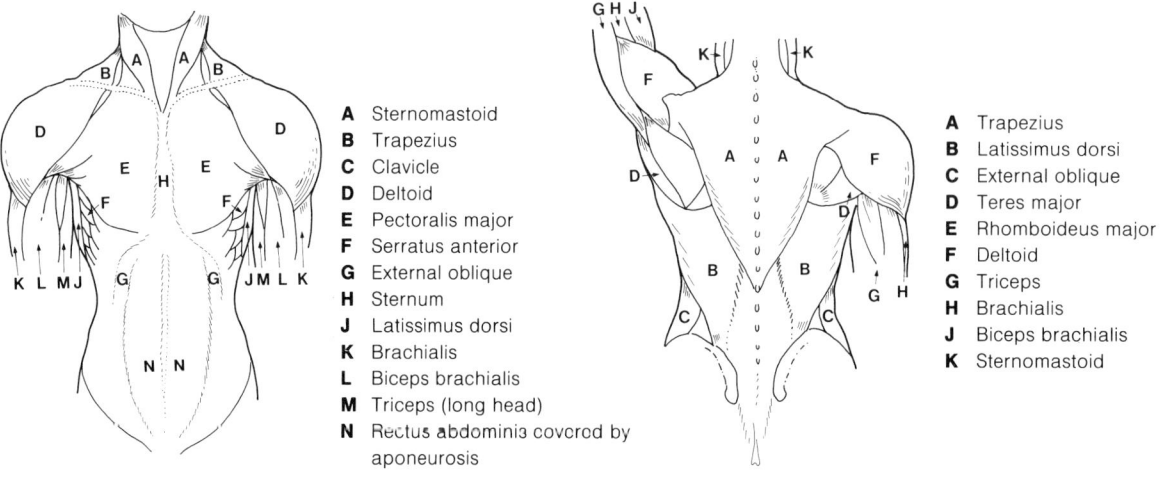

A	Sternomastoid
B	Trapezius
C	Clavicle
D	Deltoid
E	Pectoralis major
F	Serratus anterior
G	External oblique
H	Sternum
J	Latissimus dorsi
K	Brachialis
L	Biceps brachialis
M	Triceps (long head)
N	Rectus abdominis covered by aponeurosis

A	Trapezius
B	Latissimus dorsi
C	External oblique
D	Teres major
E	Rhomboideus major
F	Deltoid
G	Triceps
H	Brachialis
J	Biceps brachialis
K	Sternomastoid

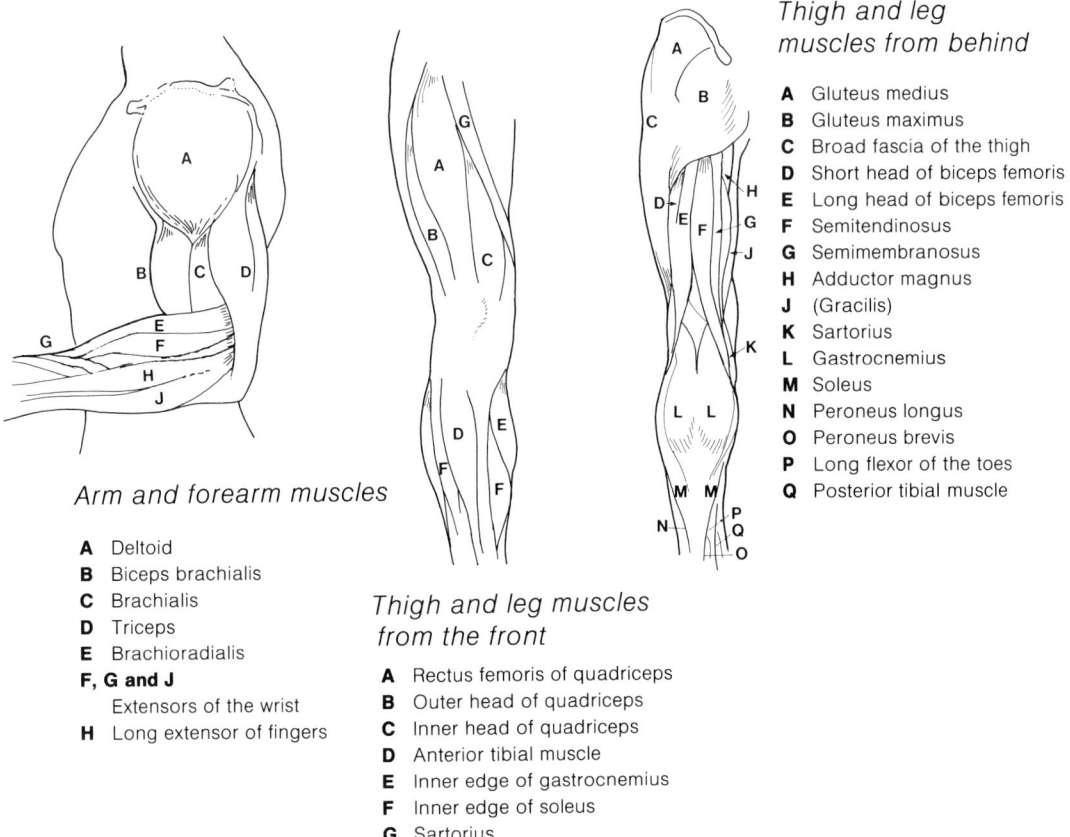

Thigh and leg muscles from behind

A Gluteus medius
B Gluteus maximus
C Broad fascia of the thigh
D Short head of biceps femoris
E Long head of biceps femoris
F Semitendinosus
G Semimembranosus
H Adductor magnus
J (Gracilis)
K Sartorius
L Gastrocnemius
M Soleus
N Peroneus longus
O Peroneus brevis
P Long flexor of the toes
Q Posterior tibial muscle

Arm and forearm muscles

A Deltoid
B Biceps brachialis
C Brachialis
D Triceps
E Brachioradialis
F, G and J
    Extensors of the wrist
H Long extensor of fingers

Thigh and leg muscles from the front

A Rectus femoris of quadriceps
B Outer head of quadriceps
C Inner head of quadriceps
D Anterior tibial muscle
E Inner edge of gastrocnemius
F Inner edge of soleus
G Sartorius

Choose the exercises to suit your own particular requirement and to ensure a balanced schedule as explained in Chapter 3 or as advised by your coach.

Power or total body exercises

Power exercises develop total body strength and speed – that quality of overall physical fitness which is fundamental to success in many sports and is so advantageous when we are coping with the many and varied demands of life in general. This power comes from the action of several muscle groups, over several joints, combining together in one explosive effort. It is the kind of power seen in sudden bursts of speed and change of direction on the football field or tennis court, in the high leaps and twists in basketball and badminton and in most athletic field events. (See also Chapter 7.)

Power exercises are not easy; the technique must be acquired gradually by using lighter weights at first so that injuries can be avoided – especially those to the small invertebral muscles. These exercises have been used successfully for years by men

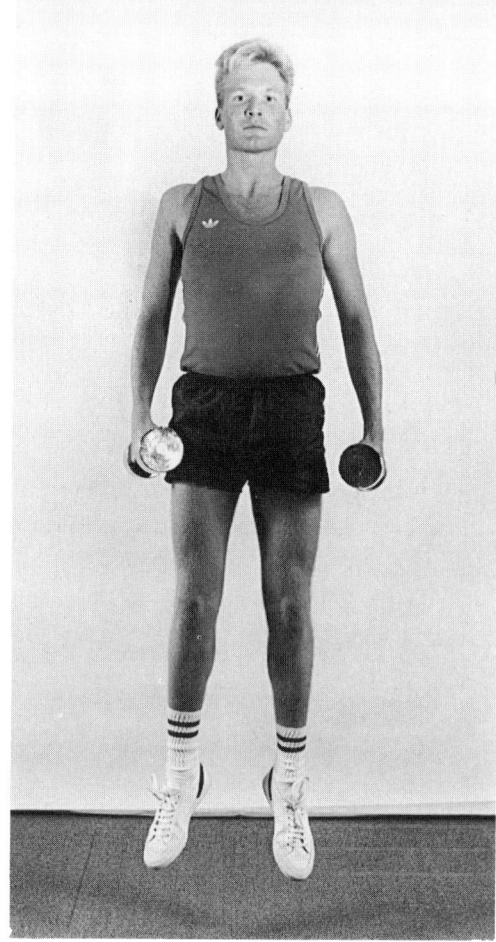

Figure 1　　　　　　　　　　　　　*Figure 2*

and women in the top ranks of athletics and sport. They are an invaluable part of any weight training programme, for they bring many muscle groups together in one forceful, highly co-ordinated action.

The squat jump (figs 1 and 2)

Muscle groups	Hip and knee extensors	*Major muscles*	Quadriceps
	Back extensors		Gluteals
			Erector spinae

This is one of the simplest of the power exercises for the beginner. Stand with one foot slightly forward of the other, lower your body into a semi-crouch position, dumb-bells held by your side. Now leap forcefully upwards, extending your legs fully and, in mid-air, changing over the positions of your feet. Try to extend your whole body, back, neck and hips. Repeat as many times as possible, whilst maintaining correct positions of body and legs.

The squat

Muscle groups	Hip and knee extensors	*Major muscles*	Quadriceps
	Back extensors		Gluteals
			Erector spinae

There are many variations of this knee-bending exercise called 'the squat' – back squat, half or partial squat – but the same safety precautions apply. Note them carefully.

1. Brace your back as straight as possible.
2. Keep the weight well back and not forward of your ankles.
3. Sink slowly into the crouch position and do not bounce.
4. Avoid bending the knees fully.

When using a heavily weighted barbell, as you will be doing in the squat, care must be taken to avoid throwing excessive strain on the back muscles, so keep the back straight and do not lean forward at the waist. The knee joint is also particularly susceptible to injury: when a heavy weight is put upon the fully flexed joint, ligaments can become stretched.

The partial squat is therefore favoured by many weight trainers.

Half or partial squat (figs 3 and 4) In addition to the safety factor, a heavier

Figure 3

Figure 4

weight can be handled if the knees are not fully bent on lowering the weight down. A bench or chair can be used to indicate the lowest point of the knee bend: stop when you feel the buttocks touching it, do not sit. This also ensures that the weight is lowered for the same distance on each knee flexion.

When rising from the squat, try to keep your body positioned correctly all the time; to avoid leaning forward think about arching your back and pushing your hips forward.

Back squat   Hold the barbell across the back of the shoulders, forearms vertical above the elbows, hands slightly away from the shoulders. Feet should be comfortably apart and heels flat on the floor. If you find it better to have your heels slightly raised then support them with a disc weight or inch (3 cm) thick board. Brace the bar firmly against the back of the shoulders. Bend at the hips and knees until the upper leg is approximately parallel to the floor. Thrust powerfully upwards, exhaling forcibly at the same time. Repeat as many times as you can.

This is a very valuable exercise but it should always be done in correct form to avoid the risk of injury. Heavy weights will be used eventually and you will need a spotter standing ready to assist in controlling the weight if you should lose your balance or find yourself unable to get up from the crouch position. In some gyms safety racks can allow you to dispense with the need for a spotter.

Front squat (figs 5 and 6)   Hold the barbell at shoulder height across the chest. Lower the body slowly into the the knee bend position, with the upper leg parallel

Figure 5   *Figure 6*

to the ground. Drive forcibly upwards to the standing position, still holding the bar firmly to the chest.

All three squat exercises develop muscle power in the range that it is invariably needed in games or in day-to-day activities. Rarely does anyone need to have the power to spring upwards in sport from the full knee bend position.

Duo Squat machine (fig. 7)   The Duo Squat exercises the complete lower body to a degree not possible with barbells and conventional equipment. The Nautilus negative cam provides the trainee with variable, balanced resistance for superior involvement of the quadriceps, hamstrings and gluteals.

Figure 7

Power curl (figs 8 and 9, overleaf)

Muscle groups	Hip, knee extensors	*Major muscles*	Quadriceps
	Back extensors		Erector spinae
	Arm flexors		Biceps brachialis

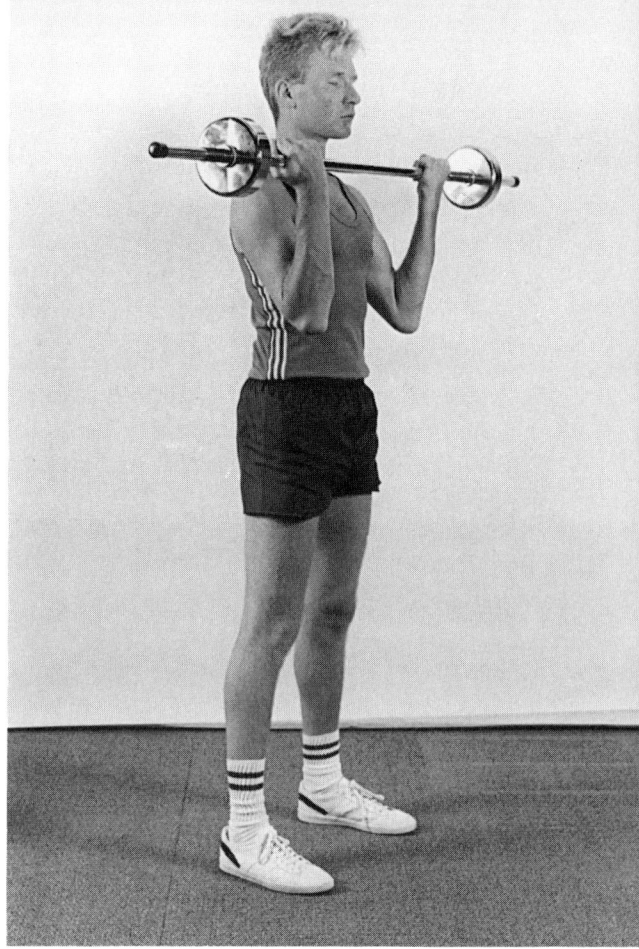

Figure 8   Figure 9

Stand with feet a little apart and under the barbell, bend into the crouch position, back straight, to undergrasp the bar (palms upwards). In one controlled movement extend your legs, hips and back, at the same time curling the bar upwards until it rests against the chest in the standing position. Lower the bar steadily to the ground in the same arc of movement and repeat. Take great care to keep your back as straight as possible during the whole of the movement to avoid strains which could prevent you from weight training for many weeks. As you will be using several muscle groups together in this power exercise, more weight should be loaded onto the bar than you would use for the simple arm curl. Hence the need for extra care in protecting the small muscles of the back.

Power press

Muscle groups	Extensors	*Major muscles*	Quadriceps
	Arm extensors		Triceps
	Arm and shoulder flexors		Biceps brachialis

Stand with barbell across the feet, hand shoulder width apart with overgrasp (palms towards the body). Bring it to the front of the chest position, dip quickly at the knees and hips with immediate recoil to push the barbell straight upwards to arm's length above the head. Do not move the feet during the thrusting upwards. Lower the barbell to the chest and from this chest rest position repeat the exercise as many times as you have set for the schedule. This is an ideal exercise because it involves the explosive contraction of many muscle groups. Initially the leg and hip extensors throw the weight to a position a little above the head and here the triceps and deltoids take over to push the weight to arm's length in one continuous movement. Many other muscle groups are also involved in stabilising other parts of the body. This is a good power exercise because more weight can be lifted with so many muscle groups involved.

Power clean (figs 10 and 11)

Figure 11

Figure 10

Muscle groups	Lower leg extensor	*Major muscles*	Quadriceps
	Hip extensors		Gluteus maximus
	Back extensors		Biceps
	Elbow flexors		Deltoid
	Shoulder abductors		

This is a much favoured exercise by both men and women for developing explosive body power as well as general endurance. It is a full body extension movement in which many multi-jointed muscles assist in its completion. From start to finish the bar is accelerated.

Crouch, gripping the bar (in overgrasp), back as straight as possible. Extend the legs and back quickly to lift the bar upwards and then, by pulling with your arms, bring the bar to shoulder level. Just before this point is reached, bend your knees slightly and bring your elbows down under the bar so that your wrists turn to support the bar on the palms of your hand at chest height. Straighten the knees to stand erect.

Duo Hip and Back machine (fig. 12)   Full-range exercise for the strongest muscles of the body, the gluteus maximus of the buttocks, is possible with this machine. Independent movement arms make certain that the resistance is equally divided between the right and left hip extensors. The Duo Hip and Back is important for improving running and jumping performance, cosmetic strengthening and firming, and hip and thigh rehabilitation.

When building your own training schedule you will naturally consider the order in which the selected exercises are to be performed and although you will have

Figure 12

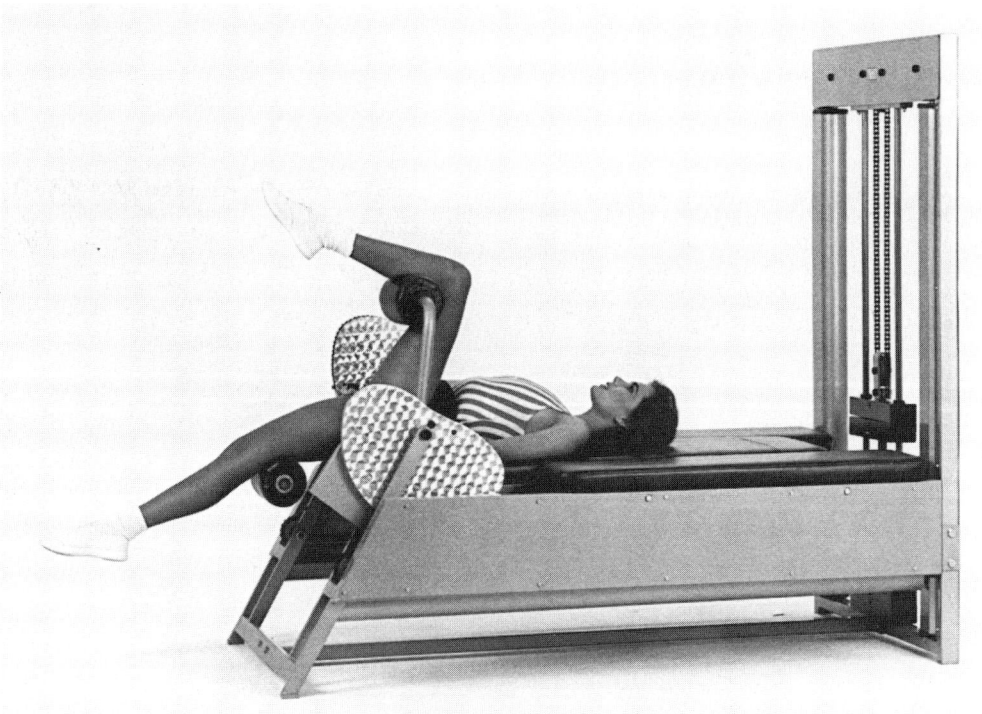

carried out the warming up and stretching exercises it would still be advisable to leave the power exercise, which is the most exhausting one, until all the other muscle groups have been exercised once. In this way you can be sure that the body had been adequately prepared.

Arm and shoulder exercises (mainly for the elbow flexors)

Arm curls, barbell (figs 13 and 14)

Muscle group   Arm flexors   *Major muscle*   Biceps brachialis

Figure 13   *Figure 14*

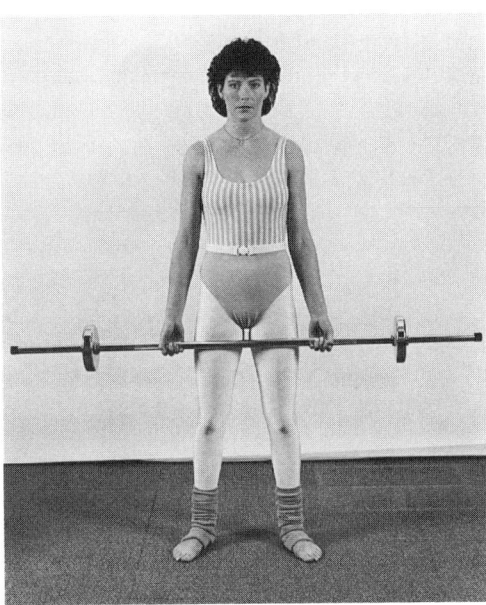 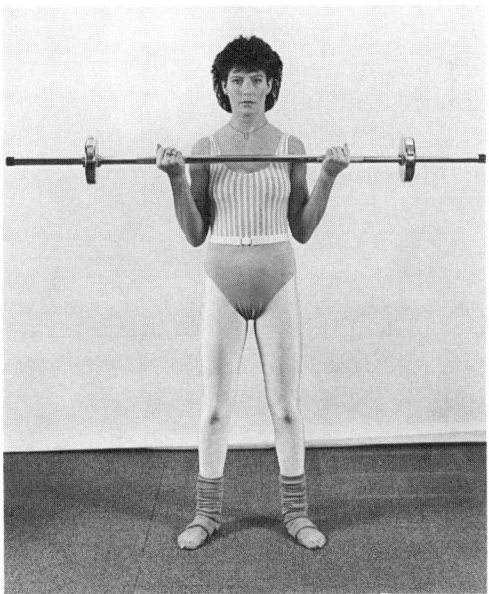

Stand with your feet a little apart, holding the barbell undergrasp, palms forward, arms hanging straight down and the bar lying across the front of the thighs. Bend your elbows to bring the bar up to the shoulder. If you want to put more work onto the shoulder flexors then push the bar forward of the body a little before bending the elbows, thereby causing more effort to be made by the anterior fibres of the deltoids. Otherwise, keep the upper arm fixed and close to the body. Return the bar in the same line to the starting position and repeat.

Reverse arm curls (figs 15 and 16, overleaf)   Grasp the barbell with overgrasp, palms towards the thighs. Tuck the elbows firmly into the waist and curl the barbell up to the shoulder.

Figure 15   *Figure 16*

Inclined bench barbell curls   Sit astride a bench with back inclined. Hold the barbell undergrasp resting across the thighs. Curl the bar up to the shoulder and back again to the start position. This modified starting position ensures that more work is done by the arm flexors, for it is less easy for other muscle groups to assist in the movement; for example, when in the standing position the back is hollowed and the hips swung slightly forward to give a little initial impetus to the weight on its upward curl.

Single arm curls, dumb-bell, supported

Muscle group   Arm flexors   *Major muscle*   Biceps brachialis

Rest the upper arm on the inclined bench. Curl the bar to the shoulder. With this starting position the action is restricted to the elbow flexors as prime movers and it is impossible to cheat by bringing other muscle groups into action.

Alternate arm curls (fig 17)

Muscle group   Arm flexors   *Major muscle*   Biceps brachialis

Stand astride, arms hanging loosely in front of the body, holding a dumb-bell in each hand. Alternately bend the right and left arms, bringing the weight to the shoulder. In this exercise other muscle groups have to work more statically, to support and steady the body during the rhythmical flexing of the arms at the elbow.

Multi-Biceps machine (fig. 18)   An unusually versatile machine, the Multi-Biceps provides biceps work in many ways –

1. Both arms together
2. Both arms alternating
3. One arm separately

– and many other permutations.

Chinning

Muscle group   Arm flexors   *Major muscles*   Biceps brachialis

Latissimus dorsi

Grasp a beam or high bar above stretch height with under or overhand grip. Pull the body up until the chin is over the bar. Return to the starting position and repeat. Make sure that a full arm extension is reached before the next pull up is attempted. For more effect on the back muscles, pull up with the bar behind the neck.

Figure 17   *Figure 18*

Upright rowing (fig. 19)

Muscle group   Shoulder abductors   *Major muscles*   Deltoid

Biceps brachialis

Supraspinatus

Use a narrow grip for this exercise. Bend the arms at the elbows and, allowing the wrist to drop, lift the barbell to chin height and lower the barbell slowly, pressing the shoulder blades together all the time.

Figure 19

Figure 20

Rowing Torso machine (fig. 20)   Often called 'the posture machine' by experienced trainers, the Rowing Torso strengthens the posterior deltoids, rhomboids, and trapezius. Exercising these muscles is instrumental for combating rounded shoulders in all age groups.

Shoulder shrugging (fig. 21)

Muscle group   Shoulder girdle elevators   *Major muscles*   Trapezius

Levator scapulae

Rhomboid

Hold a heavy dumb-bell in each hand by the side of the thighs. Raise the shoulders as high as you can and then press them backwards squeezing the shoulder blades together. Let them drop and then thrust them forwards and upwards again. Keep the arms straight throughout the exercise.

Figure 21   *Figure 22*

The same exercise can be done with a barbell, overhand grasp, hands outside the hips. Lift the barbell by shrugging the shoulders as if trying to get the shoulders to touch the sides of the face. Use heavy weights in this exercise.

Lateral raise, standing (fig. 22)

Muscle group Abductors   *Major muscles* Deltoid

Supraspinatus

Stand with feet firmly placed a little way apart. Hold a dumb-bell in each hand, palms towards the body. With straight arms lift the dumb-bells sideways to shoulder height and lower to the sides. Repeat.

Lateral Raise machine (fig. 23)   Efficient, direct exercise for the deltoids is employed in this single joint machine. Seat and handgrips are adjustable for proper support and stabilization.

Figure 23   *Figure 24*

Forward raise, standing (fig. 24)

Muscle group Shoulder flexors   *Major muscles* Anterior deltoid

Coraco-brachialis

Stand with dumb-bells overgrasped, resting in front of the thighs. With straight arms raise the dumb-bells to shoulder height and lower to starting position. Repeat.

Wrist curl (figs 25 and 26)

Figure 25

Figure 26

Muscle group Wrist flexors *Major muscle* Flexor carpi

Hold the barbell undergrasp with the forearm resting on the thigh and the wrist protruding beyond the knee. Flex the wrist upwards and towards the body. Lower the barbell as far as possible with the wrist fully extended. Repeat over the full range of movement, keeping the forearm fixed all the time.

Reverse wrist curl When the same exercise is done using overgrasp, the extensors of the wrist are exercised as prime movers and the flexors work eccentrically. Try to move the weight so that the wrist is flexed and extended as fully as possible at the end of each arc of movement.

Wrist abduction and adduction

Muscle groups Abductors and adductors

Major muscles

Flexor carpi radialis

Extensor carpi radialis longus and brevis

Flexor carpi ulnaris

Extensor carpi ulnaris

For these two exercises load the dumb-bell only at one end, stand holding the unweighted end as you would a hammer, arm fully extended by the side. Allow the weighted end to fall slowly towards the ground and then raise it again in the same arc of movement. Do the same exercise with the other wrist. For the next exercise hold the dumb-bell so that the weighted end is raised towards the elbow behind the arm. Lower the weight to the ground and raise it again to the fullest extent of the movement. Exercise both wrists in the same way. These exercises are good for sportsmen requiring extra wrist strength, as for example in tennis or basketball. (See Chapter 7.)

Exercises for the arm and shoulder extensors

Triceps extension (figs 27 and 28)

Figure 27　　　　　　　　　　　　　　*Figure 28*

Muscle group Arm extensors   *Major muscle* Triceps

Stand holding the barbell in overgrasp, hands about head width apart, with the bar resting behind the neck across the shoulders, elbows pointing upwards. Straighten the arms to press the bar to full extension overhead. Lower to the starting position following the same path of movement.

This exercise can be done with dumb-bells, exercising one arm or both at a time. Keep the upper arm holding the dumb-bell as close to the head and as vertical as possible.

Lying triceps press

Muscle group Arm extensors   *Major muscle* Triceps

Lie on the bench with the elbows pointing upwards and the bar held behind the head. Straighten the arms to push the weight into the stretch position above the shoulders and chest.

Multi-Triceps machine (fig. 29) Like the Multi-Biceps machine, the Multi-Triceps is capable of being used in many ways. By keeping the elbows in line with the rotating cams, the triceps will be stimulated to new levels of strength and fitness.

Figure 29

Figure 30   *Figure 31*

Behind the neck press (figs 30 and 31)

Muscle groups		*Major muscles*	
	Abductors		Deltoid
	Arm extensors		Supraspinatus
			Triceps

Hold the bar across the back of the neck and shoulders. Press upwards to the stretch position and lower slowly behind the neck again. Control carefully the descent of the bar to avoid bruising the back. A towel slung round the neck can act as an effective pad.

Overhead press

Muscle groups	Abductors	*Major muscles*	Triceps
	Arm extensors		Trapezius
			Deltoid

Hold the barbell across the chest at shoulder height, feet placed a little way apart. Press the barbell upwards to stretch height and lower slowly down to the start position. Keep the body upright and the knees straight throughout the exercise. The load thrown upon the triceps, pectorals and deltoids varies slightly according to the hand position and it is a good idea to alternate between a wide and narrow grasp during training sessions.

Overhead dumb-bell press (fig. 32)   You can do this exercise seated or standing. Hold the dumb-bells at shoulder height. Alternatively press the left dumb-bell and then the right to full stretch overhead.

Overhead Press machine (fig. 33)   The ideal complement to the Lateral Raise machine, the Overhead Press machine brings into action the triceps and deltoids to maximise training benefits.

Figure 32   *Figure 33*

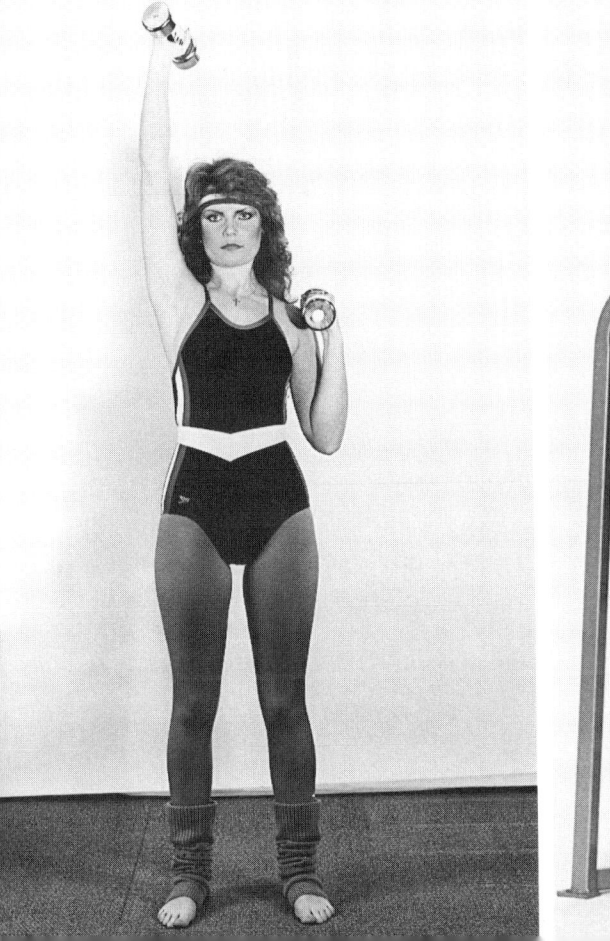

Deep press-ups

Muscle group   Arm extensors   *Major muscles*   Triceps

Pectorals

Rest the toes on a low bench or chair and support the remainder of the body weight on the hands, placed shoulder width apart on the floor. Place a disc on the flat of the back (a spotter can help here) behind the shoulders and neck. Keeping the body straight, bend and stretch the arms. If this exercise is too hard for the beginner place the feet on the floor and exercise without weight.

Shoulder extension   Lie face down on a bench. Hold a light dumb-bell in each hand and allow your arms to hang down to the floor. Keeping both arms straight, extend them alternately backwards as far as possible.

Abdominal exercises

The following exercises have been selected as being the most effective in developing abdominal strength and rehabilitating weakened muscles. For the latter purpose the back lying exercise with double leg raising should not be done as it throws too great a strain on weakened abdominals working in a lengthened condition. Exercises within the inner range, such as the trunk curls, are the most suitable for developing strong abdominal muscles with minimum risk.

It is worth noting here the differences between a trunk curl and the 'sit-up'. In the trunk curl the body is curled forward and upwards by the abdominals and hip flexors whereas in the 'sit-up' the back is kept straight and the prime movers in the exercise are mainly the hip flexor muscles.

Bent knee sit-up (figs 34 and 35)

Figure 34   *Figure 35*

Muscle groups	Hip flexors	*Major muscles*	Psoas major
	Trunk flexors		Rectus abdominis
			Obliques

Lie on your back with feet flat on the floor, hands linked behind the head, and a training partner holding your knees down. Curl your body forward until your head makes contact with your knees. When you feel strong enough to progress from this exercise then hold a disc weight behind your head and neck.

Sit-up or cruncher with upper leg raised

Muscle groups	Trunk flexors	*Major muscles*	Abdominals
	Hip flexors		Psoas major

By raising the legs so that the lower leg is resting on a bench or chair and the upper leg is vertical to the floor as you lie on your back, the trunk curl throws far more work upon the abdominals because the hip flexors are already shortened. A variation of this is the next exercise.

Trunk curl with twist, legs raised (fig. 36)   When you add twisting movements to

Figure 36

the trunk curl you are exercising the same muscle groups as above, but throwing more work upon the external and internal oblique abdominal muscles. Lie with lower legs resting on a bench or chair and upper leg vertical, hands clasped behind the head. Curl forwards and upwards, at the same time twist your body to reach with the elbow beyond the outside of the opposite knee.

Inclined curl or cruncher   Lie on an inclined bench with the feet towards the raised end and tucked under a strap. (A weight can be held behind the head.) Curl upwards to press your head close to your knees.

The Abdominal machine (fig. 37)   The muscles of the mid-section not only protect the inner organs, but are important cosmetically. This machine provides first-class exercise for most of them.

Figure 37

Abdominal retraction   This is the only exercise for developing the one muscle which all the other exercises have hardly touched – the transversalis – the broad sheet of muscle passing horizontally across the stomach keeping the viscera in place. By retracting the stomach or pulling in the wall as far back towards the spine as possible, the transversalis works against the weight of the viscera as it squeezes them into as small a place as possible. Abdominal retraction takes a little time to learn but it should be practised until a good retraction can be achieved.

Stand with the upper part of your body leaning forward at the hips and hands on the front of your thighs. Breathe out forcibly and then try to pull your stomach muscles backwards towards the spine and upwards under the rib cage, making a hollow like the inside of a dome.

Leg exercises

All the exercises for developing power exercise the leg muscles. Do remember, though, that the squat exercise should never be to the full squat position where the knee joint is being forced open as the thigh muscles act as a pivoting point on the calf. The partial squat will exercise the same muscles equally well.

The lunge (fig. 38)

Muscle groups   Knee extensors   *Major muscles*   Quadriceps

                  Hip extensors   Gluteus maximus

Hold the barbell behind the neck, feet a little apart but in line, take a pace forward and sink slowly into the knee bend position of the leading leg. Let the leading knee go no further forward than the toes of the leading foot. Return to the erect start position by pushing upwards and backwards with the leading foot and stepping back. You may take two smaller backward steps with the leading foot to get you into the starting position again.

The dumb-bell lunge (fig. 39)   This is an alternative to the barbell lunge and can be done with light dumb-bells until the technique is mastered.

Figure 38   *Figure 39*

The same prime mover muscles are involved but it should be pointed out that the lunge exercise does involve many other muscles of the body – to maintain body balance and stabilise other joints. Both for general fitness purposes and sports fitness this lunge exercise is very useful.

There are several variations of the lunge exercise. You could step forward, instead of back, to regain the starting position and some people find this easier.

There is yet another variation, as follows.

The lunge and press

Muscle groups	Hip extensors	*Major muscles*	Quadriceps
	Knee extensors		Gluteus maximus
	Arm extensors		Triceps
			Deltoid

Stand with the barbell held with overgrasp on the chest. Step forward until your forward knee is bent and directly over the forward foot. As the body is carried forward, press the barbell upwards to the arms fully stretched position above the head. Return the feet to the starting position and lower the bar to the chest. Repeat, alternating the forward leg.

Leg extension (fig. 40)

Figure 40

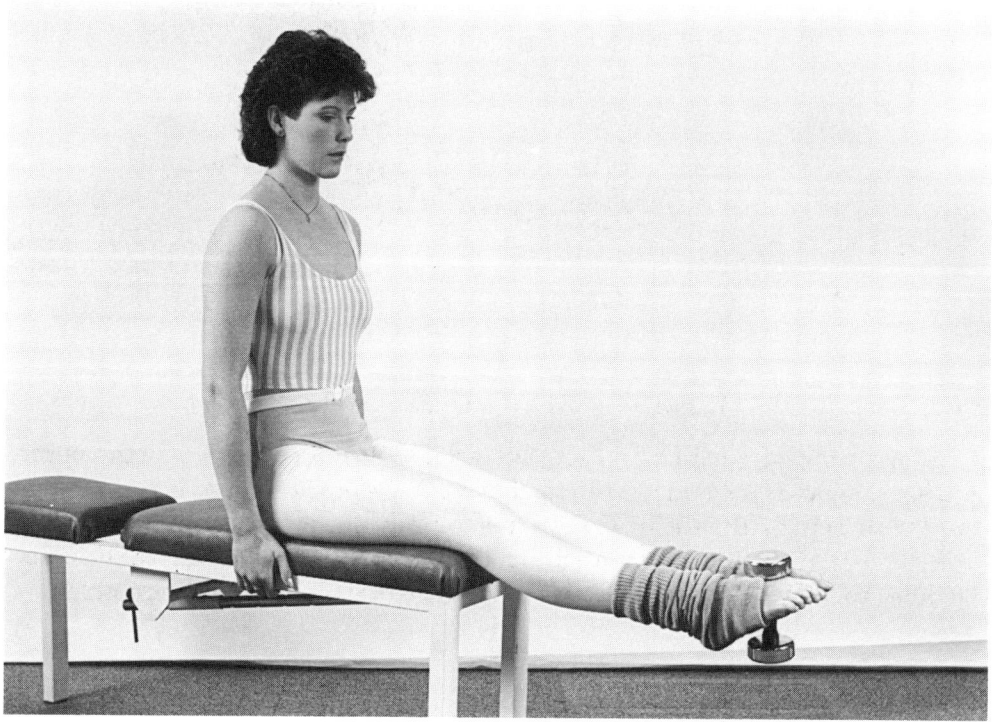

Muscle group Knee extensors   *Major muscle* Quadriceps

This exercise can be done with both legs attached to one barbell via the iron boots or with legs working singly against the resistance afforded by dumb-bells attached separately to each boot, or with dumb-bell held between the feet. Sit on a bench with legs bent to a position halfway between a right angle and the full extension. From this position straighten the legs until they are completely braced.

Leg Extension machine (fig. 41) The Leg Extension machine is designed to provide direct exercise for the quadriceps.

Figure 41

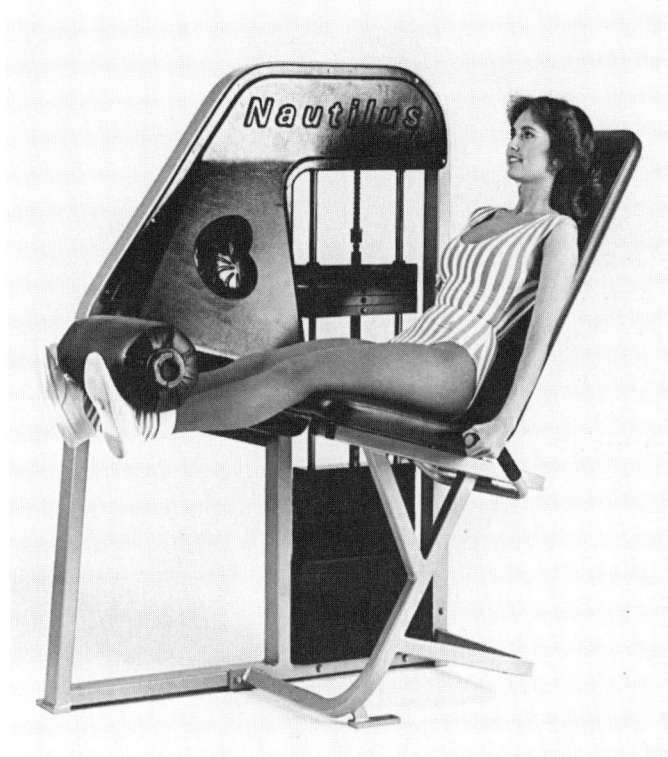

Leg abduction

Muscle group Leg abductors   *Major muscle* Gluteus medius

Lie on one side of your body with the weighted foot resting upon the other. Keeping the top leg extended, raise it slowly and lower slowly, taking care not to bruise the other ankle in the process. The abductor muscles of the outer thigh and the adductors on the inner side are difficult muscles to exercise with free weights. Machines such as the Nautilus ones are specially designed for these muscles.

Hip Abduction Machine (fig. 42)   The gluteus medius muscles on the outer hips are responsible for abducting the thighs. The Hip Abduction machine applies resistance to the outside of the thighs as the legs are spread in a deliberate manner.

Hip Adduction Machine (fig. 43)   Adduction means movement of an extremity toward the midline of the body. The Hip Adduction machine works the muscles of the inner thighs, which are responsible for bringing the legs together.

Figure 42   *Figure 43*

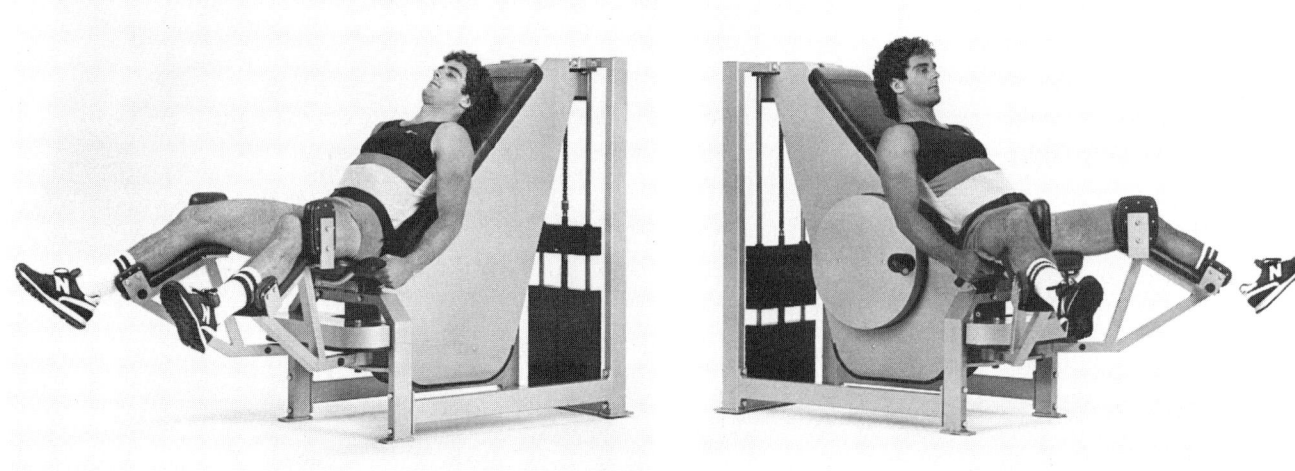

Straddle lift

Muscle group   Knee extensors   *Major muscle*   Quadriceps

Stand astride a barbell with one hand gripping the bar in front of the legs and the other to the rear, palms facing inwards. Bend and stretch the knees. Change the hand positions after each set. This kind of knee bending exercise allows the back to be kept more or less vertical. Keep the feet about eighteen inches apart.

Leg curls, standing and lying

Muscle group   Knee flexors   *Major muscles*   Biceps femoris

                                                   Semimembranosus

Stand with one hand against a support to maintain balance. Raise the booted foot until the heel approaches the back of the thigh. Lower slowly down again. A variation is the lying leg curl (figs 44 and 45).

   Lie face downwards on a bench with a weighted boot on one foot. Bend the knee backwards, keeping the knee and upper thigh firmly on the bench. Lower slowly to the extended position again. The hamstrings work strongly concentrically in

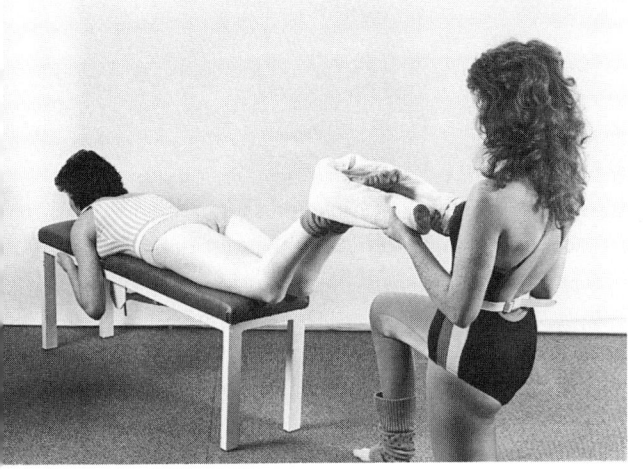

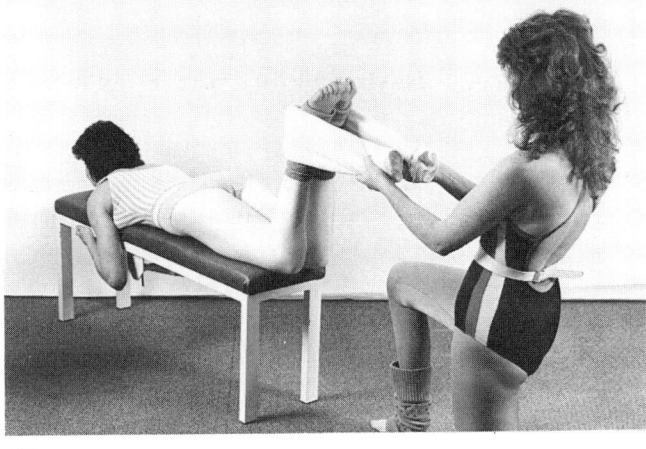

Figure 44   Figure 45

raising the weight and eccentrically in lowering in this exercise. A partner could provide resistance by holding your foot, allowing it to move more slowly.

Leg Curl machine (fig. 46)   The primary function of the hamstrings is to flex the knee and extend the hip. Besides protecting the knee, the hamstrings are important to running and jumping. Conditioning of these muscles also contributes to the appearance of the back of the thighs.

Calf raise or heel raise (fig. 47)

Muscle group   Foot plantar flexors   *Major muscles*   Gastrocnemius

                                                          Soleus

Figure 46   Figure 47

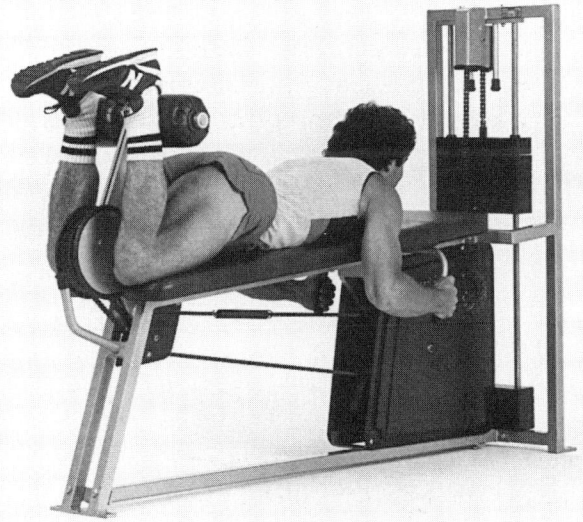

Hold a heavily weighted barbell behind your neck. Rise as high as you can on your toes to maintain a good balance throughout the movement. Lower slowly down. As a progression on this exercise place a thick board under your toes so that the heels can drop lower than the toes. Rise on the toes as high as possible and then lower the heels. Do both these exercises with a vigorous push off in order to get maximum effect.

Donkey lift (fig. 48)   This is a variation on the calf raise or heel raise. Stand with your body bent forward forming a right angle at the hips, hands resting on the bench. Have a training partner sit on your hips. Using your hands to steady your balance, raise the heels as high as you can.

In order to exercise different parts of the calf muscles do the exercises with the toes sometimes pointing straight ahead, sometimes either inwards or outwards.

Dorsal or back exercises

Most of us work every day with the back slightly bent forward – we may lean over a desk, work at a bench or sit in a car. Consequently the muscles of the back are continually working in a lengthened condition to maintain the body's equilibrium. Systematic strengthening exercises for the back muscles can compensate for this continual stooping and develop a back strong enough to avoid fatigue and the strains that are incurred by those with poor back musculature. The same exercises can be used for those wishing to improve performance in sport or athletics.

The back muscles respond well to weight training but it is important to remember this one basic principle: *never lift weights with the back bent forward and rounded.* It is from such a movement that intervertebral disc trouble springs. The short muscles and ligaments retaining the discs in position between the vertebrae are easily damaged when heavy weights are lifted in this rounded back posture. When this happens there is always the likelihood of recurring trouble. Therefore the importance of keeping the back straight when lifting cannot be emphasised too much at this stage. The exercises given below are those that work the back muscles either in their normal length or from normal to a shortened one. Exercises such as the straight leg dead lift have not been included since there is a risk in attempting to lift very heavy weights from a position in which the back does become rounded, placing great strain upon the small muscles of the back and ligaments binding the sacrum to the spine.

Trunk raising backwards (figs 49 and 50)

Muscle group   Back extensors   *Major muscles*   Sacrospinalis

Gluteus maximus

This exercise offers opportunities for progression which will bring in other muscle groups, but for the beginner the simple form of the exercise should first be

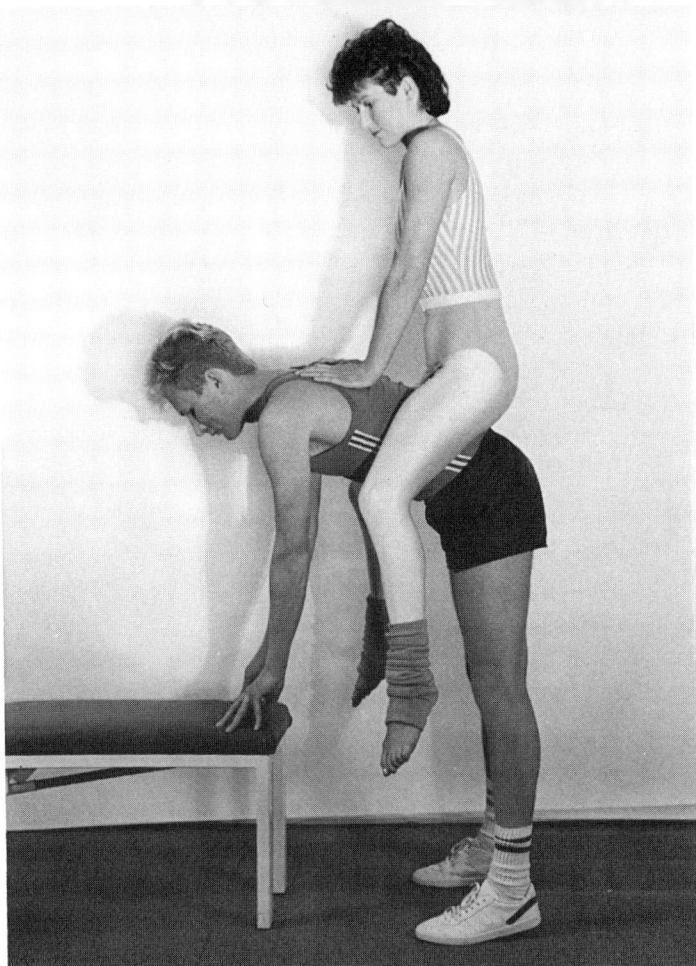

Figure 48

practised. Lie face downwards on the floor, hands clasped behind your head. Try to raise your head, spine as far as possible off the ground. Tuck the chin well in. You can increase the resistance by holding a disc weight behind your neck and head and raising your legs also. A further progression is the back raise with twist.

Back extension with twist   Lie face downwards on a bench, with a partner holding your legs firmly down. Allow the trunk to hang down over the end of the bench. With hands holding a light disc behind the neck, extend your spine as fully as possible, and twist to the right. Lower the trunk and repeat, twisting to the left.

Figure 49

Figure 50

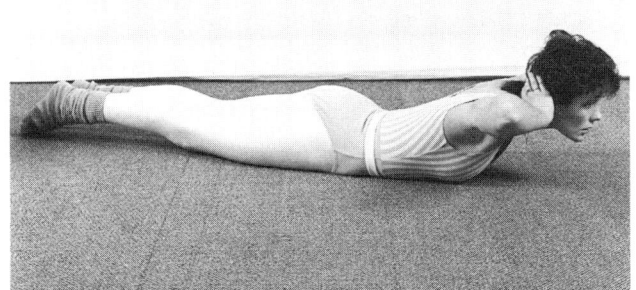

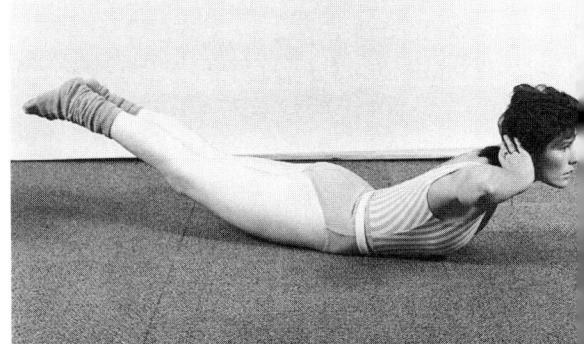

Lower Back machine (fig. 51)   It is said that there is barely a household in the world that does not have its martyr to backache, and back trouble accounts for more visits to the doctor than any other complaint. Proper exercise for the spinal erector muscles with the Nautilus Lower Back machine can prevent and help rehabilitate a large number of such cases.

Figure 51

Bent over rowing, single arm and with dumb-bell

Muscle groups	Shoulder retractor	*Major muscles*	Posterior deltoid
	Back extensors		Latissimus dorsi
			Teres major

Lean forward at the waist with one foot about half a pace in front of the other. Place the free hand upon a bench or the forward knee. Hold the dumb-bell in the free hand. Support the upper body firmly on the non-working arm. From this starting position bend and stretch the arm to bring the dumb-bell well back as far beyond the shoulder as you can manage. As a variation, you can rotate the body slightly in pulling the dumb-bell back, thus throwing work upon the oblique muscles.

Another variation would be to support your body by placing your free hand on a bench or chair. Pull the dumb-bell vigorously up to the shoulder.

Bent over rowing with barbell (figs 52 and 53)   The bent over rowing exercise is sometimes done with a barbell and the body bent forward at the hips, but a straight back is recommended. Unfortunately the 'straight back' position is not always achieved and then there is a risk of strain to the lower back muscles, especially for anyone with a pre-existing weakness there. If the knees are bent slightly during this exercise tension in the lower back is reduced.

Figure 52

Figure 53

Trunk bending sideways with barbell (fig. 54)

Muscle group   Back extensors   *Major muscles*   Latissimus dorsi

Erector spinae

Figure 54

Hold a barbell behind your neck and shoulders, hands placed as wide apart as possible, feet astride. Keeping the body erect bend sideways at the hips rhythmically to the left and then to the right. Do not load the bar too heavily in this exercise for the muscular effort involved is not only that needed to pull the weight over to the side but also that needed to check the momentum and gravitational pull so as to change the swing to the opposite direction. *Violent swinging with a heavily loaded barbell can injure the spinal muscles.*

Figure 55

Torso Arm machine (fig. 55)   This machine works the muscles of the back and the biceps of the upper arms. Work is accomplished by pulling a parallel-grip bar from above the head to behind the neck.

Chest exercises

What is it that gives a harmonious shape to the well-developed chest? The shoulders are formed mainly by the deltoids, the depth of chest by the pectorals, and the width by the latissimus dorsi running down the sides of the chest wall to the rear of the ribs and onto the attachments of the spine. The fullness and added contours are provided by the finger-like striations of the serratus magnus appearing on the front and sides of the lower ribs.

All these muscles are responsible for an important range of movements such as in pushing a heavy weight away from your body or in pushing your body away from an object.

The exercises described below are designed to work the muscles of the chest against an increasing load and to promote deep respiration. In this the mobility of the chest wall will be improved and the vital capacity of the lungs increased to cope with the additional load thrown upon the breathing system. Running, stepping and squat jumps are also good exercises for stimulating the respiratory system into increased activity. But probably the most fundamental exercise of all, for the chest, is the bench press. It is an exercise which makes use of heavy weights for strengthening and developing muscle size in the pectorals, deltoids and, to some degree, the latissimus dorsi.

This exercise is frequently recommended by women's weight training coaches as one particularly valuable in a figure-shaping routine. (See Chapter 3.)

Bench press (fig. 56)

Figure 56

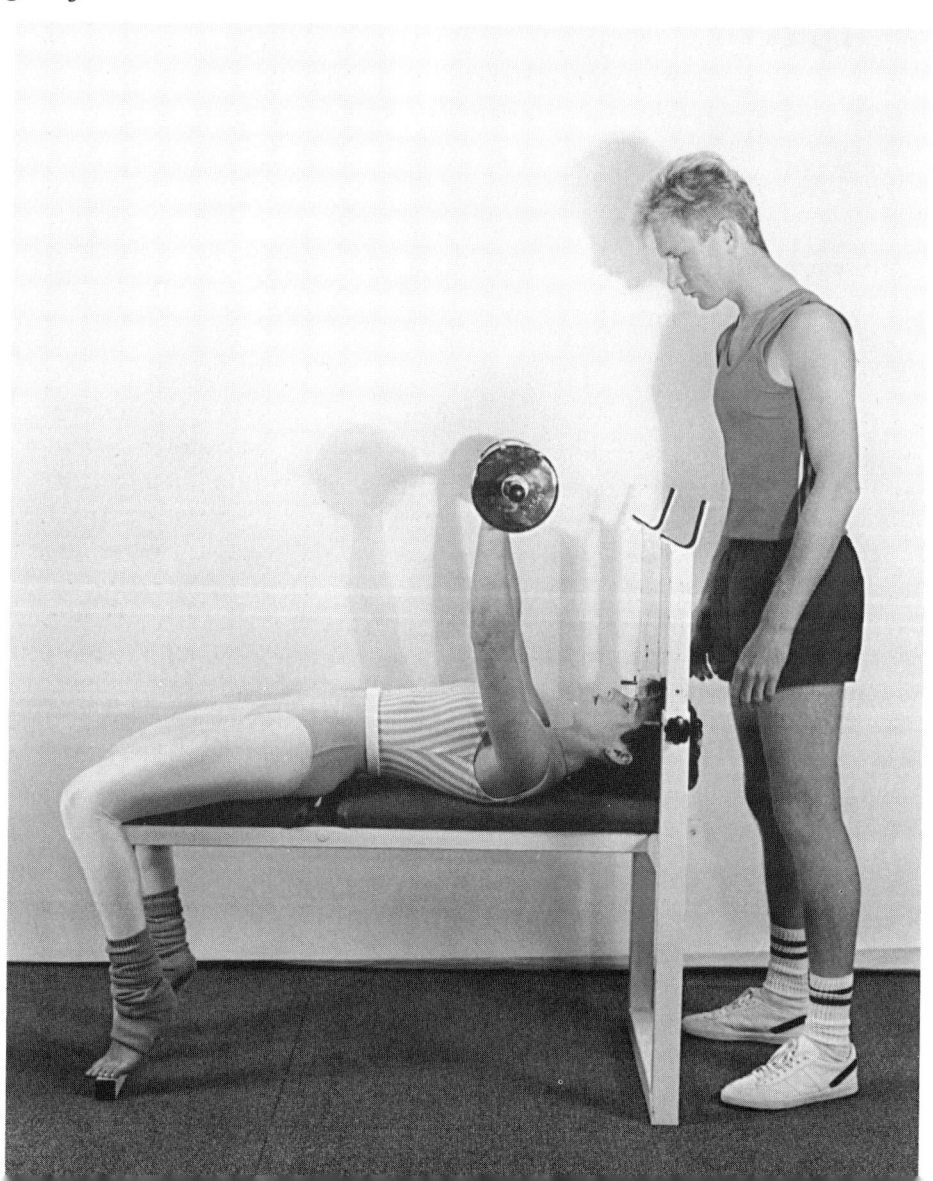

Muscle groups	Arm extensors	*Major muscles*	Frontal fibres of deltoid
			pectorals
	Shoulder flexors		Triceps

Always have a training partner standing by when attempting this exercise with a heavily weighted barbell. There have been reports of fatal accidents occurring when hands have slipped and heavy weights fallen across the throat.

Lie on the bench holding the barbell across the chest, wide grasp. Press the weight upwards to stretch height above the shoulders, keeping the arms vertical. If the hands are close together, more work is done by the triceps and less by the pectorals.

When a very heavy weight is used, take the barbell off the rack or from two training partners and lower to the chest and then press it to a straight arm position. Avoid trying to bring other muscles into the action by lifting the buttocks off the bench. Do not bring the barbell down quickly or control might be lost. Take care to follow the correct breathing technique: breathe as you press and breathe out when the arms are locked at the end of the effort. Inhale as you begin to lower the bar down to the chest again for a repeat. Exhale before pressing up again.

Bench press, dumb-bells

Muscle groups	Shoulder flexors	*Major muscles*	Frontal fibres of deltoid
	Arm extensors		Pectorals
			Triceps

The bench press is a little more difficult with dumb-bells for there is not quite the same stability as when a bar joins the two weights and consequently each arm has control of its own load. Lie on the bench with dumb-bells held above the chest. Let the arm bend until the elbows approach the floor and the dumb-bell is directly above each elbow joint. Stretch the arms upwards and then lower down to the start position. With heavy dumb-bells make sure that you have a spotter standing by in case you get into a situation where you are unable to control the weights – sometimes called 'getting pinned'. Breathe in when pressing upwards and breathe out as you reach the extended position of the arms.

Bent arm sideways raise or dumb-bell flys (figs 57 and 58, overleaf)

Muscle group	Shoulder horizontal flexors	*Major muscles*	Deltoids
			Pectorals
			Coraco-brachialis

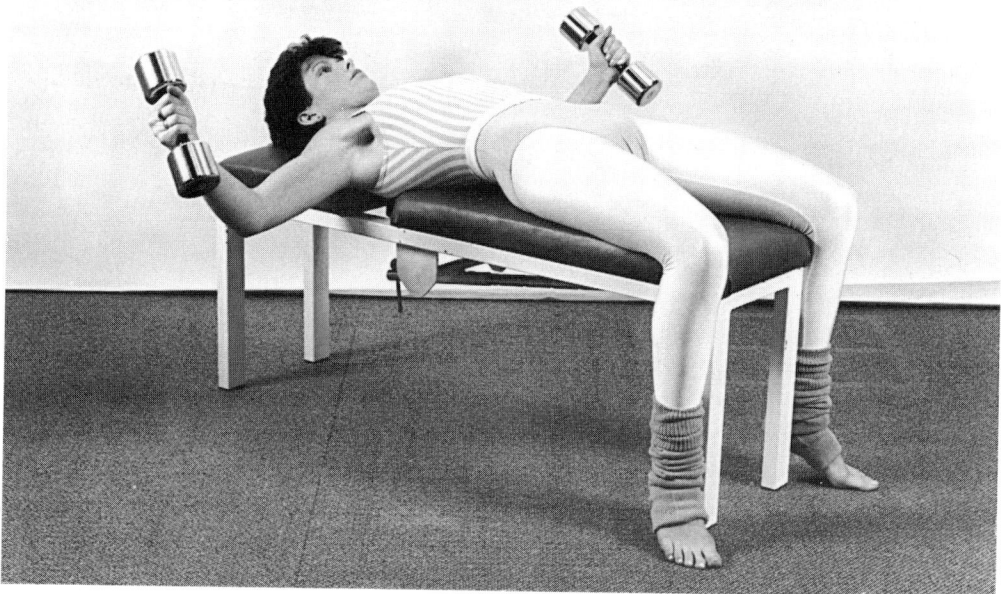

Figure 57

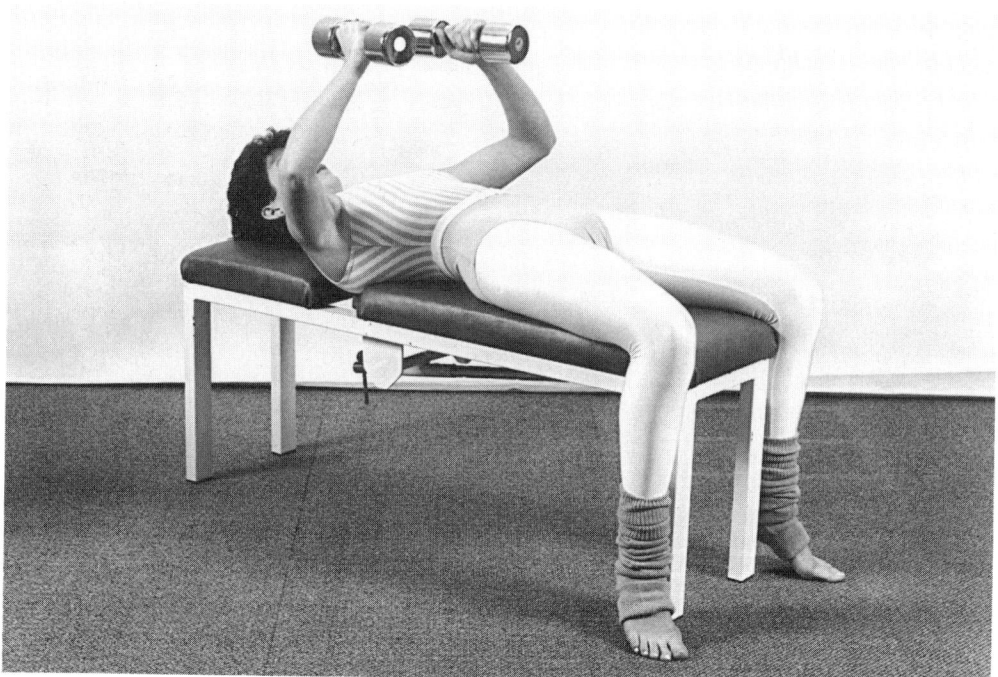

Figure 58

Lie on your back on the bench with the arms sideways and slightly bent at the elbow. Hold the dumb-bells with the thumbs uppermost. Raise the weights to the position above the chest and lower slowly down, following the same arc of movement. Breathe in as you bring the weights upwards and breathe out as you lower them slowly to the ground. Keep your arms slightly bent during the whole movement, do not lock them straight at the top position.

This is one of the best chest, shoulder and arm exercises.

Men's Chest machine (fig. 59)   The primary function of the pectoralis major muscles is to bring the upper arms down and across the torso. Function dictates design – this principle is embodied fully in the Men's Chest machine.

Women's Chest and Shoulder machine (fig. 60)   This machine allows for intense contraction of the pectorals, of particular value in the figure shaping routines.

Figure 59   *Figure 60*

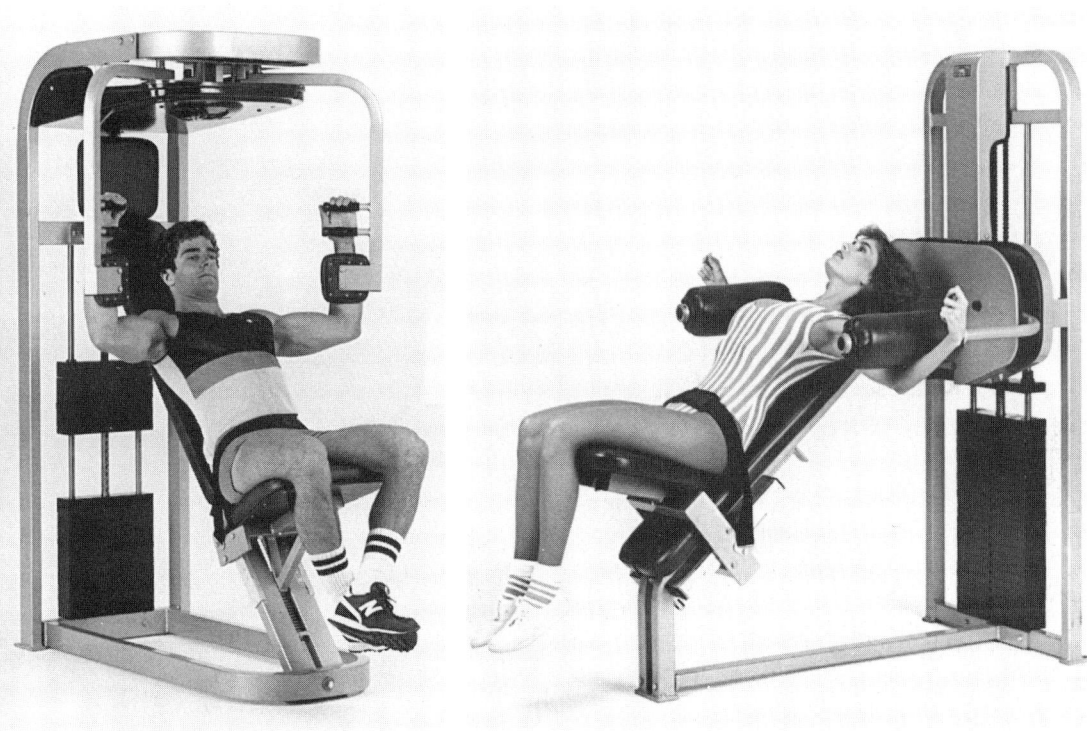

Straight arm pullover

Muscle group	Shoulder extensor	*Major muscles*	Pectorals
			Teres major
			Latissimus dorsi
			Triceps

Lie on your back on a bench with the barbell held at arm's length overhead. Slowly lower the bar backwards over the head until the weights are close to the floor at arm's length behind the head. During the lowering, the 'fanning' out of the rib cage will be felt as the weight reaches the end position. Raise the bar following the same arc on the return movement, keeping the arms straight and the hips firm on the bench. This is a first class mobilising as well as a strengthening exercise.

Double bent arm pullover (figs 61 and 62)

Figure 61

Figure 62

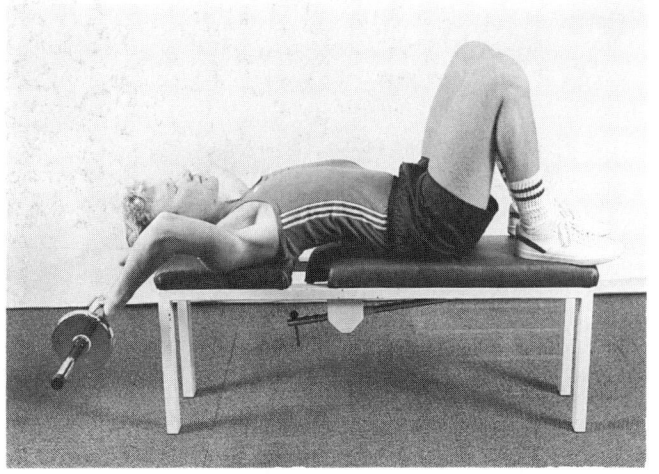

Muscle groups	Shoulder extensors	*Major muscles*	Deltoid
	Shoulder flexors		Pectorals
	Thorax		Teres major
	Arm extensors		Latissimus dorsi
			Triceps

Lie on the bench, feet flat on the floor or on the bench, head supported on the bench. Reach back behind the head then grasp the barbell with an overgrasp and, while keeping the elbows bent, pull the barbell up and over the head to a position resting on the chest. Take the barbell back over the head, keeping it close to the head with the arms bent all the time, and prepare for the next repetition.

Super Pullover machine (figs 63 and 64)   This machine provides rotary work for muscle groups of the back torso, primarily the latissimus dorsi. The latissimus dorsi is the largest and strongest muscle of the upper body. The Women's

Pullover machine allows individuals with a shorter distance between elbow and shoulder to gain maximum benefit from this rotary exercise.

Figure 63   *Figure 64*

Exercises for general endurance

General organic endurance is the ability to withstand long periods of exhausting muscular activity and to delay the effects of fatigue. It is not merely a physical condition, for it depends also upon indefinable factors such as will power, motivation, faith, morale and the ability of the mind to override the symptoms of fatigue and to carry on when the failing body indicates that it has had enough. But all other things being equal, the athlete with the well-trained circulatory and respiratory system is the one most likely to postpone the onset of fatigue and its deleterious effects during strenuous physical activity.

The heart and respiratory muscles, although different in structure from the skeletal muscles, respond to progressive resistance exercises in the same way – they become bigger and stronger. We know that running is a good way of developing general organic efficiency and endurance; so too are cycling, swimming and skipping. But it is not always possible to go for a cycle ride or swim, and so, many people make use of weight training and circuit training routines which strenuously work all the major muscle groups of the body. Remember that the leg muscles comprise two-thirds of the total muscle mass of the body and when they are exercised vigorously they make heavy demands upon the circulatory and respiratory systems.

In Chapter 8, 'Training for Stamina', further suggestions are offered on ways in which weights can be used to develop greater endurance.

Figure 65   There are many ways of applying the principle of progressive resistance to exercise, but weight training is by far the simplest and most effective . . .

Chapter Five
General principles of weight training
for athletics and sport

Success in sport and athletics is influenced by six major factors: strength, stamina, skill, speed, agility and the will to win. But the mere practice or playing of the game does not develop these physical and psychological characteristics to a high degree because during the normal course of play or competition the need for great strength or local muscular endurance arises only at infrequent intervals and furthermore, as we have already noted, the development of muscular strength depends upon increasing the demands made upon muscles through progressive overloading. Consequently a training programme for sports and athletic events needing particular strengths and endurance must include the most effective methods for developing these qualities.

Progressive weight training

Naturally, some sports and events require greater strength than others. The swimmer, canoeist and cyclist have to overcome a strong external resistance: the cupped hand and the resistance of the body through the water, the flat blade of the paddle against the water, the force of gravity acting upon the cyclist forcing the pedals up a steep hill. The external forces to be overcome in these sports clearly indicate the need for great strength and muscular endurance.

Other sports require varying degrees of strength. The footballer needs power, strength and stamina, the boxer needs strong arms and shoulders for punching power, well-developed neck and shoulder muscles to act as shock absorbers and strong legs to carry the body through many gruelling rounds. Strength requirements for some sports are not as great; flexibility, agility and power for explosive movements could be more important. Each activity calls for a certain kind of muscular exertion and capability. The experienced coach can analyse the particular requirements and construct a training regime that will enhance a player's performance.

But whatever the particular physical capability needed for a given activity, it is generally agreed that special training is necessary to develop it, in addition to match play and competition. For example, the basketball shooter or football striker who can outjump opponents has a tremendous advantage, but occasions for jumping high do not happen frequently enough during a game for the player to develop the necessary leg power and co-ordination required. Nor would actual practice in jumping develop sufficient leg power to make any real improvement in jumping height. Skill in jumping would improve and so add a little more height but the most marked improvement would be seen after strength in the leg extensor muscles had been developed through special resistance-type exercises.

Similarly, a golf club, tennis racquet, cricket or baseball bat can be swung all day without bringing about any noticeable improvement in arm strength. Swimming for hours on end will undoubtedly develop endurance but not the strength to provide the power essential for speed swimming.

It has often been said that strength is the key to success in athletics and sport and that a good strong 'un will always beat a good weak one. But what has to be decided is how much strength is needed, of what kind, and how much time should be spent on developing it when other areas of training such as skill and tactics have to be given a fair share of time.

The value of leg strength

For most sports leg strength is beneficial. When a tennis player turns suddenly and dashes to the opposite side of the court he or she is changing the direction of a projectile weighing perhaps 140 pounds or more – the body. To make such movements precisely at speed is an asset which enables a skilful player to retrieve shots which a weaker one would leave as unplayable (see also Chapter 7). But it is not only leg strength which is helping the player here; it is also strength in the muscles controlling posture.

Strength for stability

To make any stroke perfectly there is a need for stability of posture. Particularly important for this are the muscles of the back, neck and abdomen which stabilise the body in a variety of action postures, while the principal efforts of hitting, throwing and jumping are made by other muscle groups.

The golfer has an advantage over other sportsmen in that he makes his own conditions for the stroke. He has as much time as he wants to adjust his stance, consider the swing and all the factors which determine the direction, flight and speed he imparts to the ball. Yet despite the opportunity for making these preparations, unwanted body movements still occur with the beginner or weaker player and impair his shot, because of involuntary reactions of the neuro-muscular system brought about by the stimulation of the muscles making the stroke. How much more likely, then, are such distracting movements in games which involve rapid reaction to a ball or shuttlecock moving in a wide variety of directions and at different speeds. A high degree of skill is needed to co-ordinate all muscles, and strength is required to fix the body in flight or in the stretched positions from which shots are made. You may only be hitting a featherweight shuttlecock, but your back and shoulder muscles are supporting a head and trunk that weigh heavily.

The position of the head determines the way your body moves in flight. If a cat is dropped upside down, the first movement it would make would be of its head, so as to bring about the other body changes needed for regaining a landing position on its feet. Divers, gymnasts and free-fall parachutists learn how movement of the head and limbs alters body position in flight. To make a winning stroke your body must be in the best possible position for the application of force before the striking action is begun. This is accomplished by good footwork and by having the body firmly stabilised by strong, well-developed muscles. These strong postural muscles respond well to reflex stimuli and make possible shots which weaker players fail to achieve mainly because the body is in a disadvantageous position when the stroke is attempted.

When considering body movements in different positions and the muscle action involved, the pull of gravity must always be borne in mind. For example, little effort is needed to pull the head and spine backwards when standing but very much more muscular strength is needed to carry out the same movement when the trunk is stretched horizontally forward.

The more that muscle action in sport is analysed the more obvious becomes the need for general muscular strength. Even in sports which may appear less vigorous, increased strength will usually improve performance. Take rifle shooting, for example: muscular strength leads to better scores because the arms can be held steady while aim is taken. And professional ballroom dancers, both men and women, also find increased strength and stamina an asset which can be better developed by weight training than by dancing. Competitions are very long and tiring; those who can defer the distractions of fatigue are able to maintain perfect co-ordination and grace of movement for the extra critical minutes which might make all the difference between winning and being runner-up.

Phasing the training programme for sports and athletics

We have seen that each sport and athletics event is bound to have its own particular blend of the basic elements affecting success – strength, stamina, speed, agility, skill and the will to win. And we know that all this has to be considered by men and women planning the training programmes for the year. What also has to be taken into consideration is the ultimate aim and the time available. One of the first aims of any training programme will have to be general cardio-vascular fitness, which can be achieved by aerobic exercise, possibly involving the use of weights. Then the training time available will have to be allocated between practice of skills and tactics and specific strength development. For an activity which is seasonal, the emphasis placed on these elements will vary according to the time of the year. Let us then look at three phases of training: off-season, pre-season and in-season.

Coaches now tend to phase their training programmes with the seasons very much in mind, so that recognisable fitness aims are achieved within certain periods, gradually leading up to the time when a peak of fitness and performance is required.

Phase one: off-season   After a gruelling season of competition the player will derive considerable psychological and physiological benefit from a complete rest from training. But one cannot generalise on this. Some athletes rarely give themselves a break from training; decathlon champion Daley Thompson is said to have such an obsessive approach to his sport that he even trains on Christmas Day to establish a psychological superiority over his rivals. However, most athletes and sportsmen and women seem to find a complete break away from training and playing for a week or two helps them to return to hard training better than otherwise.

Hard training is what the off-season can cater for. It is a time when tough weight training schedules can be used to improve strength and power without interfering with the performance in the playing season. Time can be spent in strengthening the muscles supporting the joints which are subjected to the great strain of sudden turns on the court of field. Ankles and knee joints in particular are susceptible to early season injuries and the off-season is an ideal opportunity for this preventive training. Quadriceps muscles are known to atrophy quickly when exercise stops and for footballers who play for pleasure in the winter and have a rather long lay-off in the summer there is a lot to be said for spending a few minutes two or three times a week on leg extension exercises (see Chapter 4) to keep these muscles in good shape and strong enough to give support to the knee joint during the early part of the season.

An important aim for this period of training is the development of cardio-vascular fitness or general stamina. Running, cycling and circuit training will take up a major part of the training time.

Phase two: pre-season   This is a transitional and preparation time for a conditioning programme in which weight training can still be used advantageously but in a reduced form, concentrating on improving strength and power whilst maintaining the cardio-vascular fitness developed in phase one.

During the latter stages of phase two more time can be devoted to practice of skills and tactical moves in the game or event, and also to specific fitness training in the basic components of the performance. Thus, as the competitive season approaches, the individual's work load is cut back to allow the body to adjust to playing or performing the event.

Phase three: in-season Less time is available for weight training during the playing season, when tactical moves and skill practices tend to dominate the schedule, but there should be some time for two short sessions of weight training a week. Many sportsmen of top rank find it is beneficial for maintaining strength and flexibility gained through the more serious weight training of the earlier phases.

It will not always be possible to plan training for sport and athletics in this way. Some sports are in season all the year round, and there will be differences in circumstances of those wishing to train. Many coaches prefer to have training sessions that are clearly defined; some for conditioning exclusively and some for the practice of skills and tactics. This approach may work well with certain groups, such as in schools, colleges, military formations where attendance of all can be guaranteed every session. But for the training of amateur teams and individuals who have other commitments and cannot spend as much time on training as others, all aspects will have to be covered in one session – perhaps once or twice a week. In such a situation then the weight training or circuit training could well be the last part of the evening's session before the final cooling-down activities, skills and tactics being practised after the initial warming and stretching session.

Final thoughts

It is now generally agreed that:

1. Weight training, either with free weights or with machines, does not interfere with the patterns of complex skills needed for top-class performance in sport or athletics.
2. The stronger you are the better you perform – from the beginning to the end of the season. The outstanding games player or athlete will be the one who has the experience, skill and physical ability to deal with situations and accept opportunities as they arise at any stage of the game or event.
3. Although sporting activities can call for various degrees of strength and blends of the major elements affecting success, there should be two fundamental aims towards which training can be directed: general cardio-vascular fitness and specific strength for the particular game or event.

Suggestions on how specificity of training can be planned are given in the chapters which follow but in the end it will be the individual sportsman or woman who will discover what it is that works best, which combination of training methods produce the best results. Then training schedules can be adjusted accordingly.

Chapter Six
Training for athletics – track and field

There was a time, back in the early 1950s, when there were only two men in the whole world who could run a mile in under four minutes. They were Roger Bannister of Harrow, England, and John Landy of Victoria State, Australia. Then, through the hole in the psychological four-minute barrier broken by Bannister and Landy, came Laszio Tabori, Chris Chataway, Brian Hewson, Derek Ibbotson, Herb Elliot and many, many more. Was it all attributable to the removal of that psychological barrier, the seemingly impregnable four-minute mile? It is not an easy question to answer. Certainly the psychological aspect has to be considered but there are other reasons.

Striking progress has been made in every athletic event during the last three decades. Coaching has become better organised, schools give more time to athletics, television has stimulated interest, competition is keener and there is also that great motivator – money. Now, athletes – using the term here to include all sportsmen and women – can aim to become very rich. Winning can thrust, almost overnight, an impecunious 'also-ran' into a millionaire life-style, and that in turn can create an insatiable appetite for success. In some the dedication to training can manifest itself in an inflexibility of will and even a total ruthlessness to carve a path relentlessly to the top. And once at the top, it can be tough, mentally and physically.

In an athletic season which becomes increasingly crowded with national and international events, athletes have had to re-think their ideas on preparation. It is not quite so easy now for men and women at the top to train to a peak of performance for a few special occasions. They have to maintain a high standard over a longer period of time and, as one former Olympic gold-medallist, Chris Brasher, wrote in the *Observer* of 4 August 1985: 'It is the winter training that stores great races into the system.' You could say the same for the field events.

For this kind of fitness, then, what form should the training take? Opinions differ less with field events than with track events. Let us then consider them first.

Field events

Coaches believe that for events which involve the overcoming of some heavy resistance, strength becomes a dominating factor influencing performance. But, as no two athletes are alike, it is ultimately up to the athlete to assess critically his or her own physique, the progress required, and the ultimate goal, and then plan a programme to suit personal needs.

Training for throwing events

Training for throwing events should incorporate activities to develop and maintain all-round physical fitness as well as the specific strength and power needed for the events. Each of the four main throwing events requires power, generated in different ways, but the performance depends principally on the transfer of momentum from the body via the hand to the implement being thrown.

For example, in throwing the javelin, momentum is gained initially from the running steps up to the point when the arm is swung back to put the throwing muscles on maximum stretch before the final impelling thrust. Several things happen at once: the elastic recoil of the stretched muscles combines with the powerful contraction of the prime throwing muscles, the body rotates and the rear leg extends powerfully so that as the javelin leaves the hand, the whole body – arm, trunk and legs – extends in one explosive effort. The final power imparted to the javelin is therefore a cumulative one provided by the co-ordinated effort of all the major muscle groups of the body. Hence the need for all-round strength development as well as specific strengthening of the prime throwing muscles.

It requires precise neuro-muscular efficiency to co-ordinate the forces as they pass from one segment of the body to the next; from the legs to the hips, trunk, arm, wrist and fingers. The successful javelin thrower is the one who can make the best use of all these forces. It requires the help of a good coach to ensure that adequate strength is developed, that co-ordination is superb, and that the style adopted is the most efficient for the individual concerned.

Momentum for the discus and hammer throwing events cannot rely initially upon a run-up, and the impetus for the discus and hammer throwing events must therefore come from the rapidity of the spin turn, the rotational power of the trunk and leg muscles and the final whipping round of the body for the final delivery. Once again, the power of the whole body is unleashed in one explosive effort.

Spin techniques are not possible with the shot, and the explosive power to thrust the heavy weight forward has to be generated within the short diameter of the putting circle. Great strength of the prime muscles involved has to be developed to overcome inertia and propel the heavy shot; it is an explosive burst of power generated by rotation of the hips and shoulders, flexion of the shoulder and extension of the arm combined with the extension of the hip and knee. The final impetus is given by the wrist and fingers. The non-throwing arm is flung forcibly across the body to help with the rotation and maintain body balance. The shot putter needs tremendous power in the arms and shoulders despite assistance given by the body and leg muscles.

To sum up, then, in training for athletics throwing events, the aim must be to develop all-round physical strength and stamina, to develop the ability to co-ordinate the power exerted by all muscle groups of the body. Progress in the development of strength should go hand in hand with increases in speed and improvement in technique. A balanced programme achieving steady progress in each of these main factors is essential to final success.

Suggested weight training routines for throwing events

The winter conditioning programme should aim at developing all-round strength as well as specific strengths. The following routine is suggested for all throwers. Specific exercises for particular events are provided after this basic routine. The exercises on machines which correspond with those with free weights are equally beneficial.

1. *Overhead press* (arm and shoulder exercise: see page 55)
2. *Trunk raising backwards with twist* (dorsal exercise: see page 65).
3. *Inclined trunk curls with twist* (abdominal exercise: see pages 57–8).
4. *Squat jumps* (leg exercise: see page 38).
5. *Bench press* (chest exercise: see page 71).
6. *Trunk bending sideways with barbell* (back exercise: see page 68).
7. *Calf raise* (lower leg exercise: see page 63).

These exercises should be done with heavy weights, permitting only a few repetitions in each set.

Favourite exercises which international athletes have used and found beneficial are shown for specific events below.

Putting the shot

Although putting the shot requires great strength we should remember that it also requires speed, agility, body control and balance, and there are no specific exercises that we can say for sure will develop these qualities. Therefore many shot putters find that they can benefit in many ways from playing other games such as volleyball, basketball, handball – and even practising sprinting.

The specific exercises to develop the anterior fibres of the deltoid, the serratus anterior, pectorals and triceps muscles are given priority in the exercises but these should be combined with those suggested for all throwers above.

1. *Shoulder shrugging from back lying*. Lie on your back with a heavy barbell held at stretch height above your shoulders so that the arms are perpendicular to the ground. Push or shrug your shoulders forward to lift them off the ground and raise the weight higher. Keep the arms straight throughout the

movement. This exercise develops the serratus anterior muscle which pulls the scapular forward during the putting action. Have a spotter standing by with this exercise as you will need to use a very heavy weight for optimum effect over this short range of movement.

2. *The lunge and press* (leg exercise: see page 60).

Throwing the discus

1. *Bent arm raise from lying* (chest exercise: see page 71). This is an exercise favoured by discus throwers because it develops great strength in the pectorals and in the anterior fibres of the deltoids. The best effects are gained when the exercise is done from a bench with the arms high enough to allow the arms to fall back as far as possible before they touch the ground. These pectorals and deltoids are then worked from a stretched position. If the elbows are bent slightly then a greater weight can be handled safely.
2. *Double bent arm pullover* (chest exercise: see page 74).

Throwing the hammer

Exercises are needed for developing the rear fibres of the deltoid as well as the rhomboids and other dorsal muscles used in the final explosive effort. Clearly here again there is a need for using the power of total body exercises described in pages 37 to 45.

1. *Trunk raising backwards* (dorsal exercise: see page 64).
2. *High pulls.* Crouch with hands in overgrasp position on the bar lying across the front of the feet. Push hard with your legs to drive your body and the weight upwards so that you finish with the bar held high under the chin and your heels well clear of the ground. Slowly and well under control, lower the barbell to the ground and repeat. This exercise is very good for developing power in the legs and arms working together.

Training for jumping events

The needs of the long jumper are similar to those of the sprinter; both are aiming to project their bodies forward with maximum velocity. The high jumper, though, must concentrate all his effort into propelling his body straight upwards and over the bar. Nevertheless, although the immediate objectives are different in both jumpers, the power for the jump is generated by the same muscle groups. Specific training therefore should aim at developing strength in the extensors of the ankle, knee and hip, as well as the flexors of the thigh.

But muscles, as we have seen, rarely work independently. Prime movers work

inefficiently if the fixator and stabilising muscles are not capable of correspond-
ingly strong contractions. Therefore it would be wrong for jumpers to concentrate
entirely on developing the prime mover muscles listed above. The chest and
abdominal muscles also play a very important part in the upward thrust, as do the
muscles which move the arms. Muscles controlling posture are most important
too; long jumpers have to maintain balance during flight to achieve maximum
distance and an efficient landing.

Pole vaulters require additional strength in the arm, shoulder and abdominal
muscles. In fact, pole vaulting is probably the most difficult of all athletics events;
a high degree of speed, strength, agility and co-ordination is required. When the
hips have reached the height of the shoulders the arm muscles take over to pull the
body upwards; for this the trapezius, rhomboids, shoulder flexors, elbow and
wrist flexors contract powerfully. The legs are brought up by the hip flexors and
then the push up is achieved by strong contraction of the extensors of the wrist and
elbow; and the back extensors are used to push the body and legs even higher
before the bar is cleared. Of all the muscles involved it is perhaps the arm and
shoulder group that will require the most attention in strengthening routines.

Suggested weight training routines for jumping events

1. *Trunk curls with twist* (abdominal exercise: see page 57).
2. *Trunk raising backwards* (back exercise: see page 64).
3. *Half squats* (leg exercise: see page 39).
4. *Straight arm pullovers* (chest exercise: see page 73).
5. *Back squats* (leg exercise: see page 40).
6. *Calf raise, toes raised* (leg exercise: see pages 63–4).
7. *Inclined curls* (abdominal exercise: see pages 57–8).

Additional exercises for pole vaulters

1. *Chinning the bar* (arm and shoulder exercise: see page 47).
2. *Deep press-ups* (arm and shoulder exercise: see page 56).
3. *Inclined curls with twist* (abdominal exercise: see pages 57–8).
4. *Wrist curls and reverse wrist curls* (arm exercise: see page 51).

Track events

'The best training for running is *running* – there is no doubt about that! But an
hour or so of weight lifting a week can prove extremely useful,' say national
athletics coaches John le Masurier and Dennis Watts (*Athletics – Track Events*,
A. & C. Black, 1980). And they go on to be more specific. 'For the sprinter and
hurdler, weight training can provide extra strength and "explosiveness" in the

muscles used for starting and running at top speed. For the middle and long distance runner it can add strength to the chest, arms and abdomen to complement strength and endurance built up in the legs.'

The secret of designing a successful training programme for the running events lies in looking carefully at the components of fitness that will be required, those needing special emphasis with regard to your own physical capabilities. Then an overall plan needs to be drawn up so that the appropriate components receive special attention whilst technique to utilise additional strength and stamina is developed too. Training needs very careful planning, for, as Olympic athlete and physical education specialist, Nick Whitehead, puts it: 'Often lack of success and even injury can result from athletes practising an event before their bodies are adequately prepared for it. It could be said that they were not "fit" even though they thought they were.' (*Track Athletics*, EP Publishing, 1976.)

How are we to achieve the right kind of fitness? It is easy to agree with the principle that strong muscles are needed for the field events such as putting the shot, but not all athletes would agree that strength training with weights should form an essential part of the training for running. Runners have argued that running endurance is best achieved through running on the track, road, or across country. And up to a point they could be right. Running will certainly develop endurance and the cross country events are often used by track men as a winter conditioning programme. But endurance does not affect speed, and essentially the athlete who wins the race is the one who can run the distance in the shortest possible time; speed is the yardstick of success. And to have speed there must be power, and the basis of power is strength. Now this is the argument used by those coaches who are strongly in favour of weight training. They will talk of how the forward motion of running – as shown on a slow motion film – comprises a series of propulsive thrusts by the rear leg as it forcibly extends against the ground. The legs are brought alternately under the body to give a moment or two of support in between each forward thrust. Following this line of argument it can be seen that the rear leg is projecting the body weight – say 150 pounds – forwards and upwards in the same way as the shot putter's arm projects the shot. The difference is that the leg is propelling this heavy weight in quick succession over a period of time, depending upon the length of the race.

As the speed of the runner increases, his or her body weight is projected forwards and upwards clear of the ground for a greater distance and longer period of time until eventually, when top speed has been reached, the period of support in between each successive drive from the rear leg has become very brief.

Further observation of such a slow-motion film of the runner would reveal that his legs seem to be exerting a far greater force against the ground during the first twenty to forty metres, when the body is inclining forwards, the stride shorter and more staccato, than when the maximum has been reached and a more erect running angle of the body adopted. This could also be deduced from the holes made in the track by the feet pushing against the surface: they are more noticeable and closer together during the accelerating period. Once the runner has gained maximum speed the marks on the track are further apart and his effort is then directed towards moving the limbs rapidly and maintaining a long stride. The evidence of the slow-motion film and the marks on the track would seem to indicate that strength is needed for two purposes, first to provide the initial power to propel the body weight through the air, and secondly, to move the legs rapidly between each successive thrust. This calls for a quick swing forward, check of momentum and rapid change of direction to swing back again. There should now be no doubt that considerable strength is needed. This leaves only one question to be answered, that of how much strength runners need.

How much strength do runners need?

It is often said that the car with a big engine makes a better get-away than the one with a small power pack. This comparison is used to impress readers of athletics articles of the need for power and muscular development, but the comparison can be misleading. There is a flaw in the logic, for some high-powered cars with heavy bodies may be more sluggish in acceleration than the lighter cars geared to make better use of their power; however, with certain reservations, it can be said of both cars and sprinters that the greater the power pack the greater the acceleration.

The main power for the sprinter comes from the muscles of the thigh and buttock, but there is an important ancillary thrust coming from the calf muscles which extend the ankle, and this final vigorous push from the ankle increases the length of the stride which in itself helps to increase speed.

Many sprinters have been photographed doing arm curls and presses with dumb-bells, but the functions of the arm movements in running are vastly different from those of the legs and it is debatable whether such strength is essential for the arms. There is no external resistance to be overcome by the arms in running. The legs push against the ground, the arms against the air and the alternating rotary movements of the body. Nevertheless, many coaches have advised their runners to develop strong arm and shoulder muscles for a particular purpose. They would argue that the arm punches across the body to prevent the shoulders swinging in the same direction as the hips and causing an inefficient rolling action. Therefore it can be said that the arms are working against a considerable resistance – that of the other strong muscle groups of the body – and there is no doubt that arm movements do have a great effect upon style and length of stride. Strong back, shoulder and neck muscles steady the non-moving parts of the body and provide a fixed anchorage from which work the primary muscles used in running.

It is interesting to note how the running action of an athlete changes when strain and fatigue begin to tell. To the experienced eye of the coach the changes which occur give a clue to the additional training needed for improvement in technique and strength. The tired runner appears to allow his shoulders and neck to wobble, the head is often allowed to sink backwards. The head, being a weighty object, has a considerable effect upon body balance. When it sags backwards onto the shoulders the angle of body lean is affected and this has an adverse effect upon style and mechanical efficiency. The length of stride is cut, which causes the driving action of the legs to be reduced to prevent the athlete from falling off balance. Clearly there has got to be strength for stability, then, as well as strength for propulsion.

In the end, though, there can only be one decision to be made and that is by the athlete concerned. Once he or she feels that optimum strength has been reached then weight training can be dropped, or used for maintaining that level of strength acquired, and more time can then be spent on style, race tactics and the development of endurance.

Training requirements for different running events

Most athletes would agree that style, strength and stamina requirements vary according to the event. To compare the two extremes, marathon running is the most relaxed of styles – there is very little vigorous thrusting action to be seen in the movement of the arms and the legs – whereas sprinting is an expression of explosive and violent effort. The sprinter has to overcome inertia in the shortest possible time, and to accelerate rapidly he requires very strong muscles which respond quickly. His race may be over in ten seconds; the marathon runner need waste no effort on rapid acceleration.

Because of this difference in styles between the long-distance runner and those who run over the shorter distances, training schedules must differ too. The middle- and long-distance runner needs physical and mental stamina plus a reserve of strength to accelerate into a final spurt. Weight training can help considerably to meet these needs. Stamina can be improved in a circuit of weights and other activities, leg strength can be gained by using heavy weights with few repetitions, and mental stamina will improve during the training period as a direct result of confidence gained through battling with increasing poundages and repetitions. Ultimately this mental stamina will be self-renewing, as a result of persevering with a rigorous training routine and of noting how the body can overcome signals of distress, and also from graded experience in highly competitive and evenly matched races. The major part of the weight training routines can be done during the winter months so that once the competitive season begins there should be little need for much time to be spent on the weight training schedules.

Training for sprinting and the shorter distances should be designed to develop strength for the initial explosive thrust that coincides with the explosion of the cartridge in the starting pistol; the response must be instantaneous. The co-ordination of mind and muscle necessary for immediate response can only be acquired by an athlete who is superbly fit. Physiologists claim that progressive weight training enables the nervous system to discharge motor impulses into the muscles at a greater frequency. A greater proportion of the muscle fibres can be stimulated too. The muscle, in fact, can react more quickly and with greater force, which is just what a sprinter needs to get off the starting blocks like a bullet from a gun.

Training schedules for sprinters should therefore be directed first of all to the development of optimum strength and then towards the co-ordination of mind and muscle for the start and good style during the race. And good style will also call for supple hips. There will be a need, with most young sprinters, to increase suppleness and improve the range of movement to achieve a freely flowing action. Top-class sprinters run with a high action of the thigh in front and full extension of the hip, knee and ankle joints. Therefore flexibility should not be neglected, and then the more powerful the muscles are which extend the legs the more effective the stride will be.

Suggested weight training routines for runners

Suggestions for routines for the different types of running events are given below.

For sprinters

1. *Half squats* (knee extensor exercise: see pages 39–40). This exercise is particularly good for developing quadriceps and gluteal muscles.
2. *Trunk raising backwards* (back exercise: see page 64). This exercise makes for stability of the shoulder girdle by strengthening the dorsal and posterior deltoid muscles. Use a weight allowing about twenty repetitions.
3. *Inclined sit-ups or curls* (abdominal exercise: see page 58). The hip flexors are strengthened by this exercise and so help the runner to maintain a high knee lift.
4. *Straight arm pullovers* (chest exercise: see page 73). This exercise develops chest mobility through the fanning out of the rib cage, as well as strength in the muscles of the chest and shoulder girdle.
5. *Calf raise* (leg exercise: see page 63). Keep the knees and back straight and use a very heavy weight so that maximum repetitions are eight or ten.
6. *Step-ups* (general endurance exercise: see page 117). This is a first-class exercise for sprinters because it develops the extensors of the leg, the hip flexors responsible for the high knee lift, and also general circulatory and respiratory endurance. Use a bench or a chair at least 50 cm high.

Middle-distance runners

In addition to progressive resistance exercises with weights, some runners incorporate 'resistance running' into their winter training to improve general strength and endurance. For this purpose there is sandhill running, a succession of uphill sprints, cross country running over soft ground, running through snow and even running with a weighted belt or 'heavy hands'.

For the weight training element of their conditioning programme many athletes adopt, initially, a heavy and light routine. Some of the exercises are done in sets of heavy weights with low repetitions followed by a set of light weights with many repetitions of the same exercise. Other coaches favour a heavy routine for the early winter months with lighter weights being used as the competitive season approaches. It really is a matter for personal preference.

1. *Squat jumps* (leg exercise: see page 38).
2. *Bent arm raise lying* (chest exercise: see page 71).
3. *Inclined sit-ups or curls* (abdominal exercise: see page 58).
4. *Calf raise* (leg exercise: see page 63).
5. *Bench jumps.* Stand astride a low bench or box holding dumb-bells by the side; jump on and off the bench as many times as possible.

Long-distance runners

1. *Half squats* (leg exercise: see page 39).
2. *Sit-ups or curls* (abdominal exercise: see page 57).
3. *Burpees* (circuit training exercise: see page 117).
4. *Straight arm pullovers* (chest exercise: see page 73).
5. *Step-ups* (general endurance exercise: see page 117). This exercise is worthy of inclusion in any running schedule because of its many beneficial effects. Knee lift is improved by development of hip flexor stamina, strength is gained in the leg extensors (especially if weights are carried) and, because of the exercising of so many large muscle groups and the demands this makes on the heart and lungs, it is an excellent means of developing general endurance.

It is important to bear in mind all the time that although weight training will develop strength and endurance it is merely a supplement to training for the actual event itself. The athlete should allocate available training time so that the conditioning programme has a reasonable balance between all the different aspects of physical preparation.

Chapter Seven
Training to be tournament tough

Which sport requires the greatest fitness? It's a question that can be argued for ever and a day. Indeed, reports say that it was from one of these arguments involving a cyclist, a swimmer and a runner, that the first triathlon was born – an event which called for long-distance swimming, cycling and running. But even this testing ordeal did nothing to resolve the question. The debate continues.

Now, new statistics have been thrown into the argument. They come from the Human Performance Laboratory at Birmingham University, where Dr Craig Sharp analysed the performance of top-ranking sportsmen and women in thirty-three different sports. A series of tests, which covered most of the different aspects of fitness – cardio-vascular, respiratory, muscle speed, strength, local endurance, flexibility, and low body fat – gave points for the degree of fitness in each category. From the totals scored by each sportsman and woman, a league table was drawn up to show which of them were the fittest. The results caused a raising of eyebrows.

Right at the top were the gymnasts, just beating the stage dancers and the powerfully agile karate exponents. Occupying the bottom four places were the swimmers (long-distance), athletes (long-distance runners), rugby forwards, and table tennis players.

The performers who acted as guinea pigs for this scientific appraisal included sportsmen and women of international repute, Olympic athletes and gymnasts, national teams and squads in squash, speed skating, cyclo-cross, canoeing, fifteen top-ranking marathon runners, the Northern Dance Company and many more men and women of top calibre in the world of sport.

And what did the tests prove? In racing parlance they proved that 'there are horses for courses'. Different sports demand different kinds of fitness, general and specific. Certainly the table (opposite) was not intended to prove that the ultra-distance swimmer ploughing up and down the pool for hours on end would have been better playing ping-pong. But the table does highlight the problem of specificity in fitness training and it is understandable that many amateur sportsmen and women with great competitive attitudes often do become a little confused when it comes to getting fit for their own game. Some go entirely overboard, indiscriminately heaving weights in a frantic fitness programme, whilst others believe that just playing the game will develop all the fitness they need.

Certainly, some games, such as rugby and American football, present players with more opportunities than others for improving power and strength. In the

Scores out of ten	Cardio-respiratory fitness	Muscle speed	Strength	Local muscle endurance	Flexibility	Low body fat	Total
Olympic gymnasts	6	9	9	10	10	9	**53**
Stage dance	8	8	7	8	10	10	**51**
Karate	6	9	9	8	9	6	**47**
Swimming: 1,500m	7	6	7	9	8	7	**44**
Slalom canoeing	8	7	7	9	6	7	**44**
Squash rackets	9	7	5	8	6	9	**44**
Cyclo-cross	9	7	8	8	5	7	**44**
Basketball	9	8	5	7	5	8	**42**
Sprint canoeing	6	6	8	10	5	7	**42**
Rowing: single and pair sculls	8	7	7	9	5	6	**42**
Windsurfing	6	5	8	10	7	6	**42**
White-water canoe	7	7	6	9	6	6	**41**
Shinty	8	7	6	7	6	7	**41**
Sprint cyclist	8	10	6	7	1	8	**40**
Rowing: fours, eights	7	6	8	9	4	6	**40**
Football: 1st division	6	7	7	8	5	7	**40**
Hurling	7	7	6	7	6	7	**40**
Road cyclist	10	6	4	9	1	8	**38**
Rugby: back	7	8	5	6	5	7	**38**
Netball	8	7	5	6	5	7	**38**
Badminton	7	7	4	6	6	7	**37**
Athletics: sprinting	4	10	8	5	4	6	**37**
Lacrosse	6	7	5	7	5	7	**37**
Athletics: middle distance	8	7	4	7	2	8	**36**
Hockey	6	8	4	6	5	7	**36**
Volleyball	7	7	5	6	5	6	**36**
Speed-skating	7	7	6	6	4	6	**36**
Cross-country skiing	10	2	4	9	2	9	**36**
Tennis	5	5	6	7	5	7	**35**
Athletics: distance	9	4	2	9	1	10	**35**
Table tennis	5	7	4	7	5	6	**34**
Rugby: forward	6	5	10	5	4	4	**34**
Long distance swimming	7	2	7	10	3	1	**30**

Analysis of fitness, from the Human Performance Laboratory, Birmingham University rugby scrum, for example, leg and back muscles have to work against maximum resistance provided by the efforts of opposing players. But such strengthening activity occurs only during the playing season. To ensure optimum physical development pre-season training is essential, otherwise the season would be partly over before players reached peak fitness. Teams and individuals who win championships must be at match fitness the day the competitive programme begins. Therefore there must be some special strengthening training during the off- and pre-season, as we have seen in Chapter 5. During that time we need a basic training schedule and also a specific one.

The aim during the first phase of training for all games should be to increase general muscular strength and stamina. This is not merely as a conditioning for playing the game better but also to prevent injury. Working out with weights builds up strength in limbs and joints where there might otherwise be a weakness and a susceptibility to injury.

Basic strengthening routines for sportsmen and women

The aim during the first phase of training for all games should be to increase the general muscular strength through a well-balanced weight training schedule. Beginners should adjust the poundage to suit their own abilities, remembering that physical development depends upon progressively increasing the resistance provided by the weight rather than on the number of repetitions. Once you can do more than twelve repetitions comfortably then increase the poundage on the bar.

The exercises in the basic strengthening schedule below are numbered in the order in which they should be performed. (They are described fully, with illustrations, in Chapter 4.) Do three sets of the fixed number of exercises before passing on to the next muscle group to be worked. The schedule should be done once every other day.

1. *Alternate arm curls* (arm exercise: see page 45).
2. *Trunk curls or cruncher* (abdominal exercise: see page 57).
3. *Overhead press* (arm and shoulder exercise: see page 55).
4. *Half squats* (power exercise: see page 39).
5. *Trunk raising backwards* (back exercise: see page 64).
6. *Bench press* (chest exercise: see page 70).
7. *Step-ups* (general endurance exercise: see page 117).

More advanced strengthening routines

1. *Arm curls* (arm exercise: see page 46).
2. *Inclined curls with twist* (abdominal exercise: see pages 57–8).

3.   *Standing triceps extension* (arm exercise: see page 52).
4.   *Straddle lift* (leg exercise: see page 62).
5.   *Trunk raising backwards* (back exercise: see page 64).
6.   *Bent arm sideways raise or dumb-bell flys* (chest exercise: see page 71).
7.   *Squat jumps* (power exercise: see page 38).

Specific weight training schedules for different sports

Specific weight training schedules can prepare you physically for the particular stresses and demands involved in your chosen activity. Obviously, the levels of fitness needed will vary from one activity to another and also training will have to meet the needs of the individual. Consequently it would not be a practical proposition to set out definitive schedules for each sport. Furthermore, to do so would inevitably be repetitive, for some sports fall naturally into similar groups; for example, the fitness requirements of American football and those of rugby are similar. It seem reasonable, therefore, to consider the needs of the main groups and to give some suggested training routines for a selection of sports in each group.

It is often said that most sports can be classified into four basic categories in which the emphasis is mainly upon the following four areas.

1.   *Strength, power and endurance*
     Examples here would include football – American, Association and rugby; boxing and wrestling; hockey and lacrosse.

2.   *Stamina to sustain skill over a long period*
     Sports such as canoeing, cycling, long-distance swimming and water polo.

3.   *Body control and agility*
     Diving, gymnastics, high jumping and martial arts.

3.   *Hand and eye co-ordination plus stamina*
     Baseball, cricket, basketball, netball and volleyball, badminton, squash and tennis, golf and archery.

But immediately we put sports into such groups discrepancies spring to mind. Naturally there is bound to be a good deal of overlapping; a five-hour tennis match demands tremendous endurance and power as well as hand and eye co-ordination. Nevertheless, however arbitrary and rough the grouping of these sports may be, the examples of training schedules given below and the basic principles outlined in previous chapters should enable individuals training without the benefit of an experienced coach to build schedules that will meet their own specific needs. But first, a cautionary tale.

A word of warning

Some sportsmen and women try to develop strength for a particular sport by practising with a much heavier golf club, racquet, discus or bat, than they use in competition, believing that the increased weight will develop strength exactly where it is required. For example, baseball players and cricketers have tried to strengthen the wrist and forearm muscles by practising strokes with a bat made heavier by the insertion of lead. Sometimes success is claimed for the method but at other times the performance of the players seems to deteriorate.

Physiologists explain the deterioration by the fact that the complex pattern of the movement has been disturbed. Sports skills are usually controlled automatically by the brain. Information about the pace of the ball, direction of the wind, the position of opponents and the player is received by the central nervous system and fed to the brain which initiates reflex action. Every factor affects the power of the stroke to be made. If the weight of the racquet is altered, then the whole pattern of movement must be adjusted. For example, less power need be imparted to a stroke placed by a heavier racquet than a light one because of the increased momentum gained with the extra weight. There is no time for conscious thought when making strokes and if the reflex pattern of movement is disturbed then control is not as accurate and skill consequently deteriorates. Furthermore, if a player practises with a much heavier implement than usual then muscle groups not normally used may become involved. For example, to swing a heavily weighted cricket or baseball bat the larger muscles of the back begin to take the load off the smaller forearm muscles. The stance and the technique of the stroke is thereby altered and automatic control affected.

Conventional weight training exercises do not interfere with the pattern of complex skills and can develop all the strength a player needs.

Sports needing particular strength, power and endurance

American football and rugby   Quick bursts of power terminating in a vigorous tackle require strength for acceleration and for driving into physical contact with an opposing player. Muscle groups needing special attention are the extensors of the back, neck, hip, knee and ankle. It is these muscles that provide that forward thrust against stiff resistance. For strength in tackling, strong flexors of the arm and hand are needed, so that once a player is firmly grasped he can be held and brought down.

The style of running in American football and rugby differs in some respects from that of soccer – there is a tendency for rugby players to take shorter steps to gain quickness off the mark and to allow sudden changes of direction to take place – but the power comes from the same muscle groups as those of the soccer player; extensors of the hip, knee and ankle. To improve the power in side-stepping the abductors and adductors of the leg need some special attention. A point to remember is that these are the muscles most likely to suffer from strains and tears during the early part of the season. 'Strengthen and stretch' therefore is the dictum for pre-season fitness training.

In addition to the basic strengthening routines suggested on page 15, cross-country running, zig-zag running in short bursts on the field, dropping, rolling, recovering quickly and on running again, should be included in the pre-season conditioning programme. A useful addition to the programme would be the stamina circuit training described in Chapter 8.

Association football   The soccer player needs strength for power and stamina to maintain a very high degree of skill for the full ninety minutes plus the extra time he or she might have to play in some crucial matches. When stamina is lacking, fatigue soon begins to impair performance. Power, the combination of strength and speed, is essential for sudden acceleration and changes of direction, for jumping high to head a ball when harassed by opposing players and, of course, for shooting hard.

Heavy weights which allow a maximum of ten repetitions are used for developing strength that gives the power to generate explosive effort time after time despite fatigue. The lighter weights can be used with a high number of repetitions for developing stamina. But we must remember that there are two types of stamina; one calls for the general endurance of the heart, lungs and circulatory systems, and there is also the stamina which depends on local muscular endurance. It is the intense physical exertion which causes the heart and lungs to work maximally over long periods that brings on the fatigue we can see in a player forcing himself to run whilst nearing the stage of cramp and collapse. Local muscular endurance is needed when a group of muscles must maintain a prolonged sequence of rapid contractions. This, for example, is what happens to the calf muscles in running. They have to contract and relax in rapid succession with little time for recovery and the elimination of the waste products of fatigue. Eventually these muscles fail to respond to the nervous stimulus and further work is impossible. Sometimes the accumulation of the waste products causes the muscles to go into a painful spasm of contraction, cramp. Thus we can have local muscular exhaustion when a player is otherwise fit to carry on playing vigorously.

To achieve the general and local endurance, the strength, speed and power needed by the top-class footballer, the following forms of training are recommended:

Circuit training (see pages 111–19)
Obstacle course (see page 98)
Weight training for general strength.

Suggested weight training routine for soccer

1. *Straddle lift* (knee extensor exercise: see page 62).
2. *Trunk curls or cruncher* (abdominal exercise: see page 57).
3. *Calf raise* (leg exercise: see page 63).
4. *Trunk raising backwards* (back exercise: see page 64).
5. *Leg curls* (leg exercise: see page 62).
6. *Upright rowing* (arm and shoulder exercise: see page 48).
7. *Squat jumps with dumb-bells* (power exercise: see page 38).

Soccer today is a hard game, the rewards are richer than they were before and you have to be tough to survive. Training with weights will give you the explosive power, speed, strength, agility and flexibility needed for executing the skills and tactics of the game immaculately for ninety minutes.

An obstacle course for soccer players   The obstacle course (see below) is a purposeful form of training which brings interest and variety into the programme. The movement and agility involved develop the strength, co-ordination and local endurance needed in the game itself. Players under training can be grouped into teams of four or six and the course completed in relay fashion so that one team competes against another. The course should be made severe enough to elicit maximum effort for between thirty to forty seconds. Thus, with a team of four, the individual works flat out for twenty seconds and has ninety seconds rest waiting

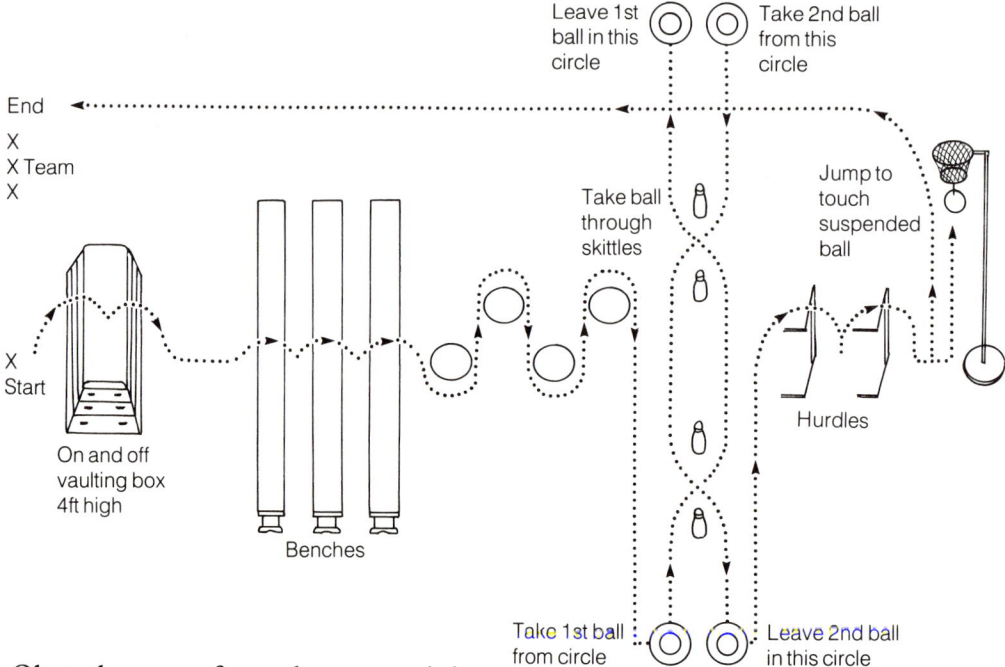

Obstacle course for endurance training

for the other team members to complete the course before starting his second lap. For players who are in a good state of training, eight or ten laps should be the initial aim. Teams can be reduced to shorten the rest period, or made more severe if players are able to complete it in less than thirty seconds.

Hockey and lacrosse 'To play hockey well today, the pre-season element of training is extremely important,' says Director of Coaching for the Hockey Association, John Cadman (John Cadman, *Hockey*, Crowood Press, 1985). 'It sets the stamina-strength base from which specific fitness for the game can be added. In line with coaches for other sports needing a high degree of strength, power and endurance, he believes that during the playing season also, specific training should be taken to maintain, and where necessary raise, the standards of the required elements of fitness.

Hockey and lacrosse players need to have the kind of fitness necessary for them to endure continuous running, frequently under pressure, to spring, to change direction suddenly and to run into a position to receive a ball or draw off a defender for seventy minutes, and also to take some punishing body contact. A strong robust body is a decided asset. Endurance for the game can be developed through long-distance running, and strength levels can be improved enormously through weight training and circuit training. Ideally, the circuit should be well-structured and performances recorded so that as times improve, the load (number of repetitions) can be increased. Suggestions for circuits and stamina training can be found in Chapter 8.

For both hockey and lacrosse, flexibility is an important aspect of total fitness – it is essential for agility and is a major factor in reducing the risk of injury.

Suggested weight training routine for hockey and lacrosse

1. *Wrist curls and reverse curls* (arm exercise: see page 51).
2. *Trunk curls* (abdominal exercise: see page 57).
3. *Lateral raise, standing* (arm and shoulder exercise: see page 50).
4. *The lunge* (leg exercise: see page 59).
5. *Upright rowing* (arm and shoulder exercise: see page 48).
6. *Squat jump* (power exercise: see page 38).

Sports which require a high degree of stamina

Cycle racing The guidelines for the racing cyclist's weight training programme are clearly set out in the authoritative book on the sport written by two former racing cyclists, Frank Westell and Ken Evans (*Cycle Racing*, Springfield Books, 1985). They write: 'One of the best ways of getting stronger is through a strictly controlled weight training programme.' They stress the need for the guidance of an experienced coach who can assess your personal needs and design a programme that will ensure that a progressive training load is thrown upon muscles to achieve the specific fitness needed, whether it be for the power of the sprinter or the stamina of the stage race rider. Although bike work will usually develop leg strength and stamina there are times when special leg power exercises can be most beneficial. Weight training is also recommended for development of the abdominals, back, arms and shoulders.

For those just starting weight training, keep the weights low enough at first to enable you to develop the correct technique of handling the equipment or machines. Use the three sets technique of ten exercises and then increase the weight that can be handled comfortably at eight repetitions. There will always be occasions when you want to draw upon your reserves of power for rapid acceleration. Training for power will involve using heavy weights as part of your programme (see Chapter 4 for power exercises). At this stage the advice of your cycle racing coach is desirable.

The demands of modern day cycle racing are such that very high levels of individual skill, tactical awareness and mental toughness are needed as well as natural ability. Time is always at a premium and you need to be sure that you are allocating it efficiently between the various aspects of training. The days are long gone when a racing cyclist could say that 'getting the miles in' was all the training anyone needed. When the advice of a coach is not readily available then make sure that you keep a careful watch on the training record in your notebook so that there is a balance between on-the-bike and off-the-bike training.

Suggested weight training routine for cyclists

1. *Arm curls* (arm exercise: see page 45).
2. *Bench press* (chest exercise: see page 70).
3. *Half squats* (power exercise: see page 39).
4. *Straight arm pullovers* (chest exercise: see page 73).
5. *Overhead press* (arm exercise: see page 55).
6. *Trunk raising backwards* (back exercise: see page 64).
7. *Bent forward rowing* (back exercise: see page 67).
8. *Power clean* (power exercise: see page 43).
9. *Inclined trunk curls or crunches with twist* (abdominal exercise: see pages 57–8).
10. *The lunge* (leg exercise: see page 59).

Stamina for cycle racing can also be developed through circuit training (see Chapter 8). As Westell and Evans say: 'Circuit training is tough. If you don't find it tough, then you aren't trying hard enough . . . Don't worry if you can't find a circuit training venue which caters specially for cyclists. It just isn't necessary, because the aim is all-round fitness, and that aim is the same for any sportsman. In fact you can reasonably benefit from mixing with people who play other sports.'

Swimming   The physical fitness required for competitive swimming varies somewhat according to the event. The emphasis changes so that for the sprint events of 100 m and 200 m power is paramount, for the intermediate events of 400 m and 800 m power and muscular endurance are needed, and for the long-distance events of 1500 m and over, general and local muscular endurance is of major importance. Each of these areas of emphasis calls for different conditioning programmes in order to achieve peak performance.

No matter how many hours a swimmer may spend in the water, his strength will not increase much after a certain level has been reached. This is because the resistance provided by the water remains the same. Therefore, the swimmer aiming for top-class competition must aim for great strength in all the muscle groups. Speed is not possible without strength. But in addition to strength the other aspects of fitness must be developed – flexibility, agility and endurance and technical ability or skill.

The well-known American coach, Dr James E. Counsilman, who has trained several outstanding Olympic champions, believes that a good deal of their success comes from carefully designed weight training programmes. For sprinters he recommends the use of heavy weights with low repetitions, and for the distance swimmers he advocates the use of low weights with many repetitions. Dr Counsilman believes that pure strength is not sufficient; strength and endurance are also of paramount importance, and consequently high repetitions with lighter weights should be the predominant method of weight training. His methods are supported by most of the world's swimming coaches, who believe in using progressive weight training schedules to develop strength + endurance.

Suggested weight training routine for swimmers

As with all the programmes suggested for sports there should be a thorough warm-up before the weights are used. This warming and mobilising routine is perhaps more important for swimmers and mobilising exercises using light weights are recommended, as shown below.

1. *Double arm circling* holding a ten-pound disc in each hand. Swing both arms backwards over the head, keeping the arms as close to the ears as possible. Change direction to circling forwards.
2. *Trunk bending sideways with barbell* (back exercise: see page 68).
3. *Standing triceps extension with barbell* (back exercise: see page 52).
4. *The lunge* (leg exercise: see page 59).
5. *Upright rowing* (arm exercise: see page 48).
6. *Squat jumps with light dumb-bells* (power exercise: see page 38).

Weight training for developing strength + endurance for the swimmer

1. *Straight arm pullovers* (chest exercise: see page 73).
2. *Pull downs* (Torso Arm machine exercise: see page 69).
3. *Chinning the bar* (arm and shoulder exercise: see page 47).
4. *Inclined trunk curls with twist* (abdominal exercise: see pages 57–8).
5. *Trunk and arm raising backwards* (back exercise: see page 64).
6. *Bench press* (chest exercise: see page 70).
7. *Power clean* (power exercise: see page 43).

Weight and repetitions should be adjusted to take into account the major areas for the particular event, as explained above.

Canoeing   For canoeing, where even greater strength is needed in order to draw the broad blade of the paddle cleanly through the water without wavering, the training schedule should include very heavy weights in the non-racing months. As the competitive season approaches lighter weights can be used and more time spent on circuit training with weights for endurance.

Suggested weight training routine for canoeists

1. *Bench press* (chest exercise: see page 70).
2. *Lying triceps press or press downs on the machine* (see page 53).
3. *Straight arm pullovers* (chest exercise: see page 73).
4. *Pull downs* (Torso Arm machine exercise: see page 69).
5. *Inclined trunk curls with twist* (abdominal exercise: see pages 57–8).
6. *Trunk and arm raising backwards* (back exercise: see page 64).
7. *Wrist curls and reverse wrist curls* (to strengthen the grip for the gripping muscles which pull the paddle) (arm exercise: see page 51).

Sports requiring a high degree of body control and agility

Men and women who participate in such sports as gymnastics, diving and the martial arts need to have their muscular reactions tuned to a response which is exactly as required for the movement involved at the particular split second of timing.

The martial arts   The martial arts are becoming increasingly popular all around the world. The exponents of karate, judo, kendo, aikido, ju-jitsu and allied arts, need to be explosively quick, to move with the speed and agility of a panther, and have the strength to throw and make counter movements against strong opponents. All this requires special training: skill, practice, weight training for strength and endurance, mobilising exercises and agility drills. On the weight training days the emphasis should be on developing power, strength and endurance.

Suggested weight training routine for the martial arts

1. *Arm curls* (arm exercise: see page 45).
2. *Inclined curls with twist* (abdominal exercise: see pages 57–8).
3. *Bench press* (chest exercise: see page 70).
4. *Power curl* (power exercise: see page 41).
5. *Back squat* (power exercise: see page 40).
6. *Straight arm pullovers* (chest exercise: see page 73).
7. *Overhead pull downs* (Torso Arm machine exercise: see page 69).
8. *Triceps extension* (arm and shoulder exercise: see page 52).
9. *Power clean* (power exercise: see page 43).

Gymnastics   The precision needed by the gymnast depends a good deal upon a high level of strength and skill. Muscular endurance, especially in the upper body region, is of paramount importance too. In fact, as we saw at the beginning of this chapter, the gymnasts are top of the all-round fitness table when every aspect of fitness is considered. Consequently the training must strike a balance between all the conditioning routines necessary to prepare the gymnast for the wide range of skills and body movements performed.

Suggested weight training routine for gymnasts

1. *Deep press-ups* (arm and shoulder exercise: see page 56).
2. *Inclined trunk curls with twist* (abdominal exercise: see pages 57–8).
3. *Half squat* (power exercise: see page 39).
4. *Trunk and arm raising backwards* (back exercise: see page 64).
5. *Calf raise* (leg exercise: see page 63).
6. *Straight arm pullovers* (chest exercise: see page 73).
7. *Squat jumps* (power exercise: see page 38).

Sports requiring hand and eye co-ordination plus stamina

Tennis   Many of the top professional tennis players have found weight training a great help in getting them tennis fit. Some use free weights, and Nautilus-type training has been increasingly used because is combines the benefits of conventional free weight training with those of the machines.

Although you don't need brute force to play tennis well, you do need adequate strength and you certainly need stamina – matches have been known to last over six and a half hours. A good tennis player needs to react quickly, change direction and recover. It is a game full of explosive reactions and agility. Carefully planned conditioning is essential and therefore the advice of a good coach can save a lot of training time.

Suggested weight training routine for tennis

1. *Wrist curls, regular and reverse* (arm exercise: see page 51).
2. *Dumb-bell flys, bent arm raising sideways* (chest exercise: see page 71).
3. *Squats* (power exercise: see page 39).
4. *Torso Arm machine* (back exercise: see page 69).
5. *Straight arm pullovers* (arm and shoulder exercise: see page 73).
6. *Trunk curls or crunches* (abdominal exercise: see page 57).
7. *Arm curls* (arm and shoulder exercise: see page 45).
8. *Bench press* (chest exercise: see page 70).

The key to successful tennis fitness training is often said to be moderation, with training aimed at developing automatic motor responses, stamina and speed.

Badminton   Pat Davis, the British Coach, has no doubts whatsoever about how fitness training can improve your performance. He writes: 'It is now accepted in all sports that regular training for strength, stamina, mobility and speed can add twenty per cent efficiency to your play as well as give you generally a greater zest for life! This is particularly true of badminton where a split second's slowness puts you on the defence instead of on the attack.' (Pat Davis, *Badminton Complete*, Kaye and Ward, 1967.)

Callisthenics, skipping, walking and running and the playing of other vigorous games can help with the basic conditioning. To play well you have to be agile and have a high degree of endurance. Like many other sports it is in the closing minutes of a competition between evenly matched players that the fitter one begins to dominate the play. There is no denying the fact that when stamina wanes so does skill. The weight training schedule shown below and the circuit training exercises given in Chapter 8 will help to develop the essential elements of fitness.

Suggested weight training routine for badminton

1. *Calf raise with toes on a step* (leg exercise: see page 64).
2. *Bench press* (chest exercise: see page 70).
3. *Back raise with twist* (back exercise: see page 65).
4. *Trunk curls with twist* (abdominal exercise: see page 57).
5. *Step-ups* (stamina exercise: see page 117).
6. *Straight arm pullovers* (arm and shoulder exercise: see page 73).
7. *Leg extension* (leg exercise: see page 60).
8. *Triceps extension* (arm and shoulder exercise: see page 52).
9. *Wrist curls and reverse curls* (arm exercise: see page 51).
10. *Behind the neck press* (arm and shoulder exercise: see page 54).

11. *Squat jumps* (power exercise: see page 38).
12. *Shoulder extension* (arm and shoulder exercise: see page 56).

Many badminton coaches also recommend the use of a weight training circuit with one or two exercises taken from each of the anatomical groups (see Chapters 8 and 4) and arranged in a sequence so that consecutive exercises do not use the same basic muscle groups.

Baseball   Baseball demands sudden bursts of strength and power but does little to develop those qualities – a feature of many sports. The body must be properly conditioned for these demands if joint strain is to be avoided and performance improved. Weight training has for many years been a feature of the training carried out by many outstanding major league players, particularly in the pre-season and off-season periods. During the season they tend to leave several days between any weight training and competitive play.

Weight training can help to develop the power for explosive muscular effort so vital to success at baseball. Emphasis is also placed on strength of the forearms and wrists.

Suggested weight training routine for baseball

1. *Power press* (power exercise: see page 42).
2. *Trunk curls or crunches with twist* (abdominal exercise: see page 57).
3. *Power curl* (power exercise: see page 41).
4. *Wrist curls, regular and reverse* (arm exercise: see page 51).
5. *Squat jump* (power exercise: see page 38).
6. *Trunk raising backwards with disc* (back exercise: see page 65).
7. *Triceps extension* (arm and shoulder exercise: see page 52).
8. *Bench press* (chest exercise: see page 70).

The ideal programme for baseball conditioning will be one combining weight training, skill drills, and plenty of running in various forms, bearing in mind the whole time that the only way to develop the strength and power needed to excel is to overload the muscles progressively, and that lifting nothing heavier than a bat and ball and a glove will not do this.

Golf   'Physical fitness is the key to top performance and success on the golf course, behind a desk, in the classroom or in the kitchen, I know it. I am absolutely confident of the fact that skill coupled with physical fitness – the ability to endure – is an unbeatable combination.' So wrote Gary Player, one of the few golf professionals to win the Grand Slam (F. Thatcher and G. Player, *Gary Player World Golfer*, Pelham Books, 1975). Since then more and more golfers, both men and women, have turned to weight training to help them through their tough schedule. But carrying a set of weights in your hand baggage is hardly practical as you go on the PGA Tour, and so to meet the demand for weight training facilities during the competitive season an enterprising company has provided a 15 m long trailer – a mobile gym – to follow the US tour. In it, at any time from 7 am until dusk, golfers can work on the exercise machines and with free weights. Almost all of the recent champions have benefited from weight training schedules specially designed for them.

'Our main purpose,' explained coach and therapist Gene Lane in *Golf Illustrated* (30 May 1985), 'is to keep players match-fit as well as prevention of injuries and rehabilitation. If we can build up the flexibility and strength of the prominent golfing muscles, particularly those of the Rotator Cuff – the four muscles of the shoulder – then we should get fewer injuries. If they do get hurt then we should get them back playing more quickly.'

Suggested weight training routine for golfers

1. *Lateral raise* (arm exercise: see page 50).
2. *Power clean* (power exercise: see page 43).
3. *Trunk raising backwards with disc* (back exercise: see page 65).
4. *Trunk curls with twist* (abdominal exercise: see page 57).
5. *Wrist curls, and reverse curls* (arm exercises: see page 51).
6. *Upright rowing* (arm and shoulder exercise: see page 48).
7. *Trunk bending sideways with barbell* (back exercise: see page 68).
8. *Power clean* (power exercise: see page 43).

Squash   'You have to be tremendously fit in squash simply in order to survive, let alone win,' writes Jonah Barrington, world champion for six years (*Murder in the Squash Court*, Stanley Paul, 1982). Barrington's coach, Nasrullah Khan, did not believe in isolating any particular muscle group; he would say, 'You must be strong everywhere,' and by this he meant mentally as well as physically. And one good method of developing total body fitness that Nasrullah knew was weight training. Another method he favoured was running. Barrington did both. He also realised that what the top Pakistani players did was worth heeding: playing squash for at least two hours every day. Barrington believes this helped him but he also believes that it is necessary for squash players to involve themselves in other training activities, to bring variety into the routine and to prevent them from thinking of the squash court as a prison! 'After a time, the squash court can be claustrophobic and the walls begin to close in, so it's important to ring the changes, to be able to go away from the court and keep fit in another area.'

Training for squash is an individual matter; there is no one system that would suit everybody but there is one aspect to the training that nearly all squash players would agree upon: the need to train under pressure. The speed, endurance and intensity of effort involved in squash at the highest level has to be developed through very hard work under pressure over a long period. As Barrington himself puts it: 'The trainee squash player has not simply to work hard; he or she must be put through the wringer.'

Suggested weight training routine for squash

There are some players who do not need much weight training for the upper body but they need it for the thighs and calves, while others might have strong legs but are weaker on top. Consequently the schedule below is one which would meet with the requirements of those squash coaches, like Nasrullah Khan, who believe that strength must be developed in every part of the body. This can be done by following the schedule below, and the general endurance, mental toughness and conditioning for work under pressure can be achieved from circuit training against the clock (see Chapter 8).

1. *Wrist curls* (arm exercise: see page 51).
2. *Calf raise* (leg exercise: see page 63).
3. *Trunk curls* (abdominal exercise: see page 57).
4. *Trunk raising backwards* (dorsal exercise: see page 64).
5. *Arm curls* (arm exercise: see page 45).
6. *Partial squat* (power exercise: see page 39).
7. *Reverse wrist curls* (arm exercise: see page 51).
8. *Press behind the neck* (arm and shoulder exercise: see page 54).
9. *Trunk bending sideways with barbell* (back exercise: see page 68).
10. *The lunge* (leg exercise: see page 59).
11. *Bench press* (chest exercise: see page 70).
12. *Power clean* (power exercise: see page 43).

This routine is a rigorous one. Do not attempt to complete all the exercises if signs of physical distress become evident. Progress under pressure, yes; but sensibly and safely too.

Cricket You can never tell with cricket. One day you can score a century, take five or six wickets and hold a couple of brilliant catches in the slips. The next day you can be out for a duck, see your bowling smashed all over the ground and drop a dolly when your concentrations wanes fractionally. There's no other game quite like it for unpredictability. And that's all part of the game's fascination and appeal. Despite the unpredictability of the game, though, there is something that can be done to reduce the risks of having one of those bad days; it boils down to time spent in practice with a good coach and time spent getting really fit for the game. To play cricket well you have to be really fit.

The need for fitness is explained by the most successful and exciting all-round cricketer of modern times, Ian Botham, in this way: 'Concentration is the most vital quality for a cricketer. And if you are tired and out of breath because you are not fit, you will not be able to concentrate hard for longer than an hour. Fatigue plays tricks with your mind and takes it from the match. I am sure professional cricketers are fitter now than they ever have been – just as I think fielding standards are also at an all-time high. The two are linked. Players field better because they are more mobile – and mentally they are more alert because they are fit.' (Ian Botham, *Cricket*, Cassell, 1980.)

The basic fitness required by the cricketer is for general stamina, the ability to maintain a high standard of skill from the beginning of play in the morning to six o'clock at night. And you have to be tough to survive. Cricket is a hard game. It demands courage as well as skill. 'It takes a special kind of person to face up to demonic bowlers trying to exploit the trace of fear in a batsman.'

In bowling, the muscles which take a lot of strain are those of the groin, the hamstrings and those of the back and shoulder. All these muscles need special care in stretching and strengthening. Some fast bowlers go through a special stretching routine immediately before going on to the pitch. They rest one leg on the shoulders of a shorter player and slowly straighten the leg to its full extent. England physiotherapist, Bernard Thomas, was said to do this with Bob Willis before every match. Ian Botham follows the same stretching routine.

'The Ian Botham of women's cricket', as Sarah Potter was described in the *Sunday Times* of 5 May 1985, is another great believer in fitness training. Sarah, a left-arm fast bowler for England, is also a county hockey player. 'They are both bat and ball games,' she explained, 'demanding hand and eye co-ordination.' In the autumn between the end of the cricket season and the beginning of the hockey she trains with weights. So do many cricketers. Fred Tyson, National Coach of the Cricket Association, recommends a routine which includes nine exercises for all-round development as shown below.

Suggested weight training routine for cricketers

1. *Military or overhead press* (arm and shoulder exercise: see page 55).
2. *Arm curls* (arm and shoulder exercise: see page 45).
3. *Half or partial squat* (power exercise: see page 39).
4. *Inclined curls* (abdominal exercise: see page 58).
5. *Overhead pull down* (Torso Arm machine: see page 69).
6. *Leg extension with weighted boot* (leg exercise: see page 61).
7. *Leg curls* (leg exercise: see page 62).
8. *Wrist curls, regular and reverse* (arm exercise: see page 51).
9. *Bench press* (chest exercise: see page 70).

All-round tournament toughness

We have seen that although conditioning for top-class sport has to be specific, there is one common factor: the need for stamina, physical and mental. It can be developed through various forms of pressure and circuit training, to which we now turn.

Chapter Eight
Training for stamina

Sportsmen and women who reach the heights of physical achievement invariably possess more than skill and muscular ability; they have a marked degree of mental toughness too. It is a quality ingrained in every champion, partly bred in the bone and partly developed through a long conditioning process. There is no easy way to the top; it is a hard grind in which muscles have to be worked to their limits in a rigorous training programme and the mind taught to push the body on despite discomfort and feelings of fatigue.

When the mind becomes accustomed to rejecting the alarm signals flashing from tired muscles wanting to rest, distress symptoms fade and the body, which always seems to underrate its own ability, forges ahead to greater feats still. The mountaineer can force his way through driving snow and blasting wind to conquer the peaks, the long-distance runner fight to the finishing tape, the fast bowler put every ounce of effort into each delivery and the tennis champion play his opponent into the ground. They know they can carry on for they have done it before, learned to ignore the distractions of physical distress, pain and fatigue. It is this quality, this complex blend of physical and mental endurance, that distinguishes the star from the average performer.

The knowledge gained from the experience of rigorous endurance training develops self-confidence which in turn encourages the athlete to make additional demands upon his body even though his lungs feel fit to burst and his heart is pounding in his ears. Half the battle is won when the mind believes that its body is capable of doing what it is asked to do and more.

The chief aim of stamina training is to improve circulatory and respiratory efficiency. Rigorous exercise for the large muscle groups of the body is the way this is usually achieved for, as muscles burn up energy, increasing demands are made for the fuel and oxygen carried to active muscles by the blood. The lungs work harder to re-oxygenate it and the heart pumps more rapidly and strongly to drive the oxygen-laden blood to tiring tissues.

The leg muscles, which comprise two-thirds of the body's total muscle mass, are those usually exercised most thoroughly in endurance training. Long-distance running, without doubt, is one of the best ways of developing general organic efficiency and endurance but when, for practical reasons, running is not possible, there are alternative exercises such as those used in the circuit training schedules described on pages 114–17.

Middle- and long-distance runners who have broken world records in recent years have employed a combination of weight training, circuit training and running. Sometimes the running may take the form of fast laps of a track with intervals of slow laps between the fast ones, running up steep soft sandhills, or jogging over fells. Mountaineering has also been used by well-known international athletes in training for events needing endurance. These, and similar activities, create demands upon the circulatory and respiratory systems which consequently develop to cope with the tasks asked of them.

Endurance training can be boring; because long periods of training are necessary to build stamina, variety must therefore be introduced into the training schedule. The conditioning programme needs to be varied enough to keep the mind alert and each individual interested in his own reactions. Gradually, as a result of regular endurance training, changes take place in the body. The heart muscle responds to overload in the same way as the skeletal muscles, by becoming bigger and stronger. Hypertrophy, as this growth is called, is a natural and beneficial development which enables the heart to pump a greater volume of blood into the arteries with each beat; its stroke volume is raised. Consequently, the resting heart rate drops. That of a long-distance runner in training may be in the lower forties whilst that of an untrained man is usually between sixty and seventy beats per minute. The same sort of reaction has been found in tests done on animals – the more active ones have larger hearts than those that don't run about so much. Greyhounds, for example, have larger hearts than pet house-dogs of the same size.

The enlarged heart, satisfying normal requirements with a slow resting beat, has a greater reserve (cardiac reserve) to call upon when the demands of strenuous exertion need to be met by an increase in blood flow. Furthermore, whilst the heart rate of the untrained man must increase rapidly to cope with any additional physical activity, the heart of the trained man uses its capacity for maximal dilation and the rate does not need to increase as much in meeting the same output requirements.

Another way in which the circulatory system improves through training is by developing the capability of opening up more capillaries within working muscles. This allows energy fuel and oxygen to be more readily available and it also facilitates the elimination of waste products of fatigue.

Prolonged periods of stamina training bring corresponding improvements in the respiratory system. Vital capacity, the difference in volume between maximum expiration and maximum inspiration, improves after a regular exercise programme. By extreme comparison, the vital capacity of people who are incapacitated by injury and are bed-ridden decreases. Although there is conflicting evidence on the value of the vital capacity figure as a general index of fitness, there is little doubt that in certain activities, such as long-distance running and swimming, a large vital capacity is highly desirable.

With increased vital capacity comes a reduction in the resting rate of breathing due to the large absorptive surface of the lungs and also to the improvement in pulmonary circulation, both of which contribute to a more speedy and efficient exchange of carbon dioxide and oxygen. The highly trained athlete may have a resting respiratory rate as low as eight times a minute as compared with eighteen times a minute of an untrained man.

For the performance of the same given amount of work, experiments have shown that the athlete who has undergone rigorous stamina-type training takes in a smaller volume of air than the untrained man. This seems to indicate that stamina training develops a more efficient system for the oxygenation of blood. More oxygen is absorbed from a given volume of air breathed.

One of the most popular and purposeful forms of stamina training is the one that we know as circuit training.

What is circuit training?

As the name implies, it is a form of training that involves going round a sequence of exercises (usually between six and twelve) one after the other with a short pause between each. Individuals do a set number of repetitions at each exercise in thirty or sixty seconds until they come to the first exercise again and start a second lap.

The exercises are specially selected so that a fixed amount of effort is required in each one. This might be measured by the number of repetitions, the resistance or load provided for the muscles to work against, or a time factor for the completion of the whole schedule. Exercises must be simple and involve very little skill. Two or three circuits, or laps of the exercises, constitute a training session, and as training progresses the improvement in strength and stamina may be seen in the increase of repetitions, the heavier poundage used or the decrease in the overall time taken for three laps of the circuit.

Circuit training is an aspect of physical education which is almost a subject in itself and teachers are advised to read the standard book on the subject, *Circuit Training*, written by the originators of the idea, R. E. Morgan and G. T. Adamson (Bell, 1961).

Preparing a circuit

Circuit training is used mainly to develop general endurance and basic strength but if a high degree of strength is required then heavier weights must be used with fewer repetitions, according to normal weight training practice. With circuit training, exercises can be selected to give a special bias to particular aspects of fitness depending upon the aim of training and the physical condition of the trainee. Coaches can devise circuits to develop strength, power, endurance and even skill under stress.

For all-round physical development, exercises are usually selected to work all of the major muscle groups, such as the arm flexors, arm extensors, leg, dorsal, abdominal and chest groups. The circuit should also include exercises for general respiratory and circulatory endurance. The best exercises for this type of development are those involving massive movements and calling for great effort from the leg muscles (which comprise two-thirds of the total muscle mass of the body) and as many of the other muscles of the body as possible. Typical exercises for the development of cardio-vascular-respiratory endurance are the burpees and step-ups exercises (page 117).

No single exercise can develop both strength and endurance equally well at the same time, and it is for this reason that general fitness training circuits should include some exercises which call for many repetitions with comparatively light resistance to develop endurance and some with a weight resistance that allows only a few repetitions in order to increase muscular strength.

Training rate

When circuit training was first introduced the task at each exercise was fixed for each individual by his or her performance of maximum repetitions at a separate testing session in which there was a short rest and recovery period in between every exercise. One-half or two-thirds of a trainee's maximum repetitions for each exercise was the task usually set for training. He was then given a card to be completed according to his test performance. But during the last few years circuit training has changed considerably. More exercises have been added to the basic ones recommended by Morgan and Adamson and further fields of profitable application have been found.

The individualised form of training described above found few advocates on the Continent. Simpler systems were necessary in order to allow groups of varying ability to train regularly and at the same time within minimal administrative interference. Experience showed that it was rarely necessary to measure each individual's performance and set his training task accordingly. Instead, broad bands of training tasks were fixed to suit the approximate ability of participants.

When they can complete the circuit without undue exhaustion, progress can be made by:

1. Increasing the repetitions in each exercise, or
2. Increasing the resistance provided by the exercise, or
3. Reducing the time taken for the complete circuit.

When the first method of progression is used the increased task should be done, if possible, in the same time as the original circuit. Exercises may be made more severe by adding weight or altering the starting position so that more body weight provides the resistance to the working muscles – as, for example, when the feet are raised in the press-ups exercise, more weight is thrown upon the arm extensor muscles. The simplest method of making progress with a group of trainees who are at a similar stage of fitness training, such as may be found in a soccer club or basketball team, is by reducing the time taken to do the complete circuit. The equipment for each exercise remains the same and each individual tries to reduce his own time for the schedule. Sometimes the equipment can be duplicated so that a harder circuit can be done by the stronger trainees and a less severe one by those who are not quite so fit. Some clubs and schools have 'green', 'blue' and 'red' circuits with trainees progressing through the easier grades to the hardest.

Organisation of circuit training

Until individuals are well acquainted with circuit training schedules it is worth while having a large numbered picture for every point on the circuit. Pin drawings or enlarged photographs, with two or three clear instructions printed below, can save a lot of explanations to trainees who are not clear where to go next and what to do. Photographs are better than drawings for showing clearly the correct position for each part of the exercise.

Once the intensity of exercise has been fixed for each group then the coach or teacher gives the signal to start. A whistle blast is effective for starting and stopping work. Initially it is safer to use a 20-second stint of work followed by 20 seconds for rest and movement to the next exercise station on the circuit. With fitter athletes the exercise period can be extended to 30 seconds. The duration of exercise depends also upon age (special care should be taken by those over forty), physical condition (exercise for people with infections can be hazardous) and length of circuit (in a circuit of fifteen exercises a 20-second exercise period is advisable).

When circuit training is taken in schools it is usually advisable to leave the circuit for the end of the period so that pupils finish on it as a climax to the lesson. They will usually be sweating profusely and ready to retire to the showers. They will certainly not be in a receptive mood for learning new skills. Fatigue distracts the class from the coach and half-hearted efforts would be made. On the other hand, there is something to be said for practising skills after a circuit training session, especially in those sports which demand the maintenance of a high degree of skill even when players are very tired. A team trained in this way can face 'extra time' more confidently after a gruelling ninety minutes of cup-tie football.

There is always a temptation for performers to make straight for the apparatus when it is set out as a circuit. Coaches and teachers must insist on a thorough warm-up session before starting strenuous exercise.

Fourteen or fifteen is the best age to introduce circuit training in schools. Both boys and girls are beginning to pay more attention to their physical development and comparative strength. Progress, which is readily seen, is a good incentive, and in boarding schools voluntary evening training has proved to be a popular activity. Care, however, should be taken to avoid overstrain. Children will want to keep up with their classmates, and there is a danger here for the weaker pupil.

The attraction of circuit training

Circuit training provides a positive stimulus to further effort because progress can be measured so easily. Children, in particular, like to have targets to aim at and gain enormous satisfaction from achievement. The strong and the not quite so strong can derive just the same gratification in watching the improvement in their performance.

With voluntary circuit training, individuals can work according to their own schedule and yet feel they are part of one group working together.

Circuit training exercises

Nearly all load-resisting exercises are suitable for inclusion in a circuit but some are more suitable than others. The basic principles to guide selection are that the exercises should:

1. Require little skill and be known to the class.
2. Be easily measured in terms of time or repetition.
3. Induce fatigue within half a minute.
4. Affect large muscle groups.
5. Be easily duplicated so that bottlenecks do not arise from waiting for a turn on the equipment.
6. Give the particular bias to the circuit according to the degree of strength and endurance required.

For the arm and shoulder flexors

1. *Chinning the bar or beam*
    With the beam above stretch height and hands in overgrasp or undergrasp, bend and stretch the arms. Overgrasp is better when development of the back muscles is required. This exercise is particularly effective for the development of latissimus dorsi, posterior deltoids, rhomboids and trapezius. Undergrasp with the elbows forward allows more work to be done by the pectorals, biceps and brachialis, as well as the other heaving muscles.

2. *Fall hanging, chinning* (for younger groups)
    Beam at shoulder height, overgrasp, hand shoulder width apart, body at right angles to the arms, legs and body hanging obliquely under the beam

supported by heels and arms, bend arms to raise the chest to the beam. Lower the beam to hip height to progress to more difficult work.

3. *Heave jumping* (for younger groups)
   Beam above stretch height, jump to overgrasp and bend the arms to look over the beam and lower to drop on to the feet again. Repeat with another jump.

4. *Rope climb* (with or without the use of the feet and legs).

5. *Arm curls* (elbow flexor exercise: see page 45).

6. *Upright rowing* (shoulder flexor and abductor exercise: see page 48).

For the arm and shoulder extensors

1. *Press-ups*
   Front support position with hands shoulder width apart, body and legs in line, supported by the hands and toes. Arm bending and stretching. The exercise may be made easier by resting the hands on the wall-bars or a box. The higher the legs are raised above the hands the greater the work for the arm extensors.

2. *Lying triceps press* (arm and shoulder extensor exercise: see page 53).

3. *Jump dips* (for young groups)
   Rest the body on top of the parallel bars, jump to press the arms straight and momentarily support the body between the bars. Lower the feet to the floor and repeat with a jump.

4. *Press behind the neck* (arm and shoulder extensor exercise: see page 54).

5. *Overhead press* (arms and shoulder extensor exercise: see page 55).

For the dorsal muscles

1. *Trunk raising backwards with medicine ball*
   Prone lying, ball behind the neck. Lift the head and chest as high off the floor as possible.

2. *Trunk raising and lowering*
   Prone lying across the top section of the box horse, feet held by partner. Trunk raising and lowering.

3. *Heave with bar behind head*
   Wide overgrasp of the bar or beam above stretch height. When the body is raised so that the bar passes behind the neck there is a greater dorsal effect.

4. *Trunk raising backwards* (back exercise: see page 64).

For the chest muscles

1. *Deep press-ups*
    Front support position with hands resting on benches placed shoulder width apart. Bend the arms so that the chest dips between the two benches. Press up again. The wider the benches are and the deeper the chest dips between them, the greater is the load placed on the pectoral muscles.

2. *Rope climb*
    The rope-climb activity can be climbing a single rope a given number of times, climbing a single rope without use of the feet, climbing one rope and then travelling sideways to come down the rope at the far end of the group or climbing two parallel vertical ropes without using the feet.

3. *Rope-ladder climb without use of feet*

4. *Bench press, wide grip* (chest exercise: see page 70).

For the abdominal muscles

1. *Trunk curl* (abdominal exercise: see page 57).

2. *Inclined curl* (abdominal exercise: see page 58).

3. *Inclined curl with a twist* (abdominal exercise: see page 58).

4. *Curl sit-ups with legs raised*
    Back lying with legs raised almost at right angles and supported against a wall. Sit up to touch the knees with finger tips.

5. *Double leg lift over towel or vest*
    Place vest or towel on floor and sit with legs over the centre of it. Lift both legs together and place on one side of the vest and then on the other. Count the number of times the heels touch the floor on both sides of the vest in thirty seconds.

For the leg muscles

1. *Half squats*
    Stand in front of low vaulting box or chair, lower down to a half knees-bend position to touch the top of the box with buttocks and raise up until the legs are almost straight. If the legs are kept slightly bent throughout, the exercise is more taxing because the leg muscles have no opportunity to relax momentarily by allowing the body weight to rest on the joints and ligaments as can occur when the body is balanced in an upright posture.

2.   *Bench jumps*
     Stand astride a low bench holding a medicine ball in each hand. Jump on and off the bench as many times as possible within the prescribed time limit.

3.   *Calf raise* (lower leg exercise: see page 63).

4.   *Shuttle run*
     Place two skittles ten yards apart. Run from one to the other and back again as many times as possible within half a minute.

For general endurance

Most of the exercises for general endurance are also leg exercises. They provide vigorous work for the large muscle groups of the body.

1.   *Step-ups*
     Stand facing a vaulting box top or bench. Step on to the box with the left foot leading and then step down again, leading with the left foot. Step up and down as many times as possible within thirty and later fifty seconds. Weight may be carried by those who are really fit.

2.   *Squat jumps* (power exercise: see page 38).

3.   *Leg thrust*
     In the front support position place the left foot forward so that the weight of the body is supported by hands and toes. On the count of one, thrust the left foot backwards and bring the right leg forward under the body. At the count of two, change the positions of the legs again.

4.   *Straddle jumps*
     Stand holding a medicine ball under each arm, leap in the air and land with the right foot forwards and the left backwards. On alternate counts of 'one,two, one,two' change the positions of the feet with a jump each time.

5.   *Burpees*
     This is a four-count exercise. Stand, drop into crouch position on 'one' with hands flat on the floor. Thrust both legs backwards into the front support position on the count of 'two'. Jump the legs forward on the count 'three' and stand up on 'four'.

A suggested circuit for 13 to 18-year-olds

Instructions for performing the exercises described below may be found in Chapter 4 or in this chapter, above. Trainees should note that the circuit provides a complete programme in that all the major muscle groups are exercised systematically. It is a simple circuit without complicated movements and it can be made progressively more demanding according to the state of an individual's fitness. It is also compatible with the needs of a wide variety of trainees, no matter what level of training or experience they have in progressive resistance exercise.

1. *Burpees* (see page 117).
2. *Press-ups* (see page 115).
3. *Squat jumps* (see page 38).
4. *Trunk raising backwards with medicine ball* (see page 115).
5. *Inclined curls* (see page 58).
6. *Shuttle run* (see page 117).
7. *Chinning the bar or beam* (see page 114).
8. *Bench jumps* (see page 117).

Circuits for sport

Specially designed circuits are often used in the conditioning programmes of sports teams, for the higher the standard of play the greater are the demands made upon players. To succeed in today's highly competitive and highly paid world of sport, men and women must be supremely fit. No longer – as we have already noted in the weight training chapters – will match play itself suffice to promote the high level of specific fitness required for success.

The first requirement for an effective training circuit for a particular sport must be for the coach to identify the specific areas of fitness requiring attention. To illustrate the point let us look at the game of basketball. The attributes of a good player are stamina, speed and leg strength, for these qualities of fitness have great significance in the game. The best way of developing specific fitness, we know, is through exclusive conditioning periods. It is in these sessions that circuit training has come into its own. A good circuit for basketball would include the following six activities:

1. *Step-ups* (see page 117).
2. *Press-ups* (see page 115).
3. *Sprints or shuttle run* (see page 117).
4. *Chinning the beam or bar* (see page 114).
5. *Squat jumps* (see page 38).
6. *Trunk curls* (see page 57).

Modifications can be made to suit particular sports. For example, volleyball teams were advised by Don Anthony, former Chairman of the Amateur Volleyball Association of Great Britain, to do their press-ups on the ball itself to develop finger strength, because strong fingers made the volley action better. To develop spring, the volleyball players had to jump upwards to grasp the high bar for their chinning exercise. The ability to jump vertically upwards in volleyball is essential for to jump upwards and *forwards* near the net would mean that the chances of touching the net – and thus fouling – are high. In such ways circuits can be designed to suit the particular needs of a sport.

Safety considerations

There is a certain amount of risk in circuit training, especially when free weights are used, because movements tend to be done more rapidly and this often means with less attention to good style. Teachers and coaches find it advisable to stress this point to trainees at frequent intervals to minimise the risk of injury.

Furthermore, because of the speed with which trainees pass from one exercise station to another there is also the risk of apparatus becoming unsafe. Careful supervision is essential to ensure that equipment is properly assembled and that weights are securely fastened onto bars. A weight dropped onto a foot can easily fracture the small bones and keep an individual off training for weeks.

Trainees should be encouraged to work so that the rhythm of each exercise is regular and not laboured. They should breathe freely and avoid closing the glottis when performing the more strenuous movements.

Circuit training is designed to exercise the whole body in such a way that the rate and depth of respiration is increased considerably and that perspiration is profuse, but there should be no signs of real physical distress. Coaches should look for signs of excessive breathlessness or nausea and stop anyone pushing himself or herself too far and beyond the barriers of safety.

Training – as with any sport – sometimes exposes inherent weaknesses such, as, for example, in the spine. Trainees should be made aware of such possibilities and that if there is an unaccountable and troublesome pain anywhere after training (other than natural stiffness), they should seek medical advice. This said, however, when a training schedule progresses gradually in poundage and repetitions there is little need to fear any harmful effects.

Obviously, circuit training is tough. And if those taking part do not find it so then the severity of the tasks should be progressively increased in one of the following ways or in a combination of them: by reducing the time limit, increasing repetitions, increasing the difficulty of the exercise by adding weights or by altering the starting position, or by doing an extra circuit.

We know that the mind can be educated to withstand the discomfort of fatigue and that muscles can be trained to a pitch of efficiency performing remarkable feats, but the ultimate achievement in endurance activities depends upon the will to succeed, to win or survive when the situation is desperate. The motivating force is of paramount importance. Ambition, anger, fear and pride can push the body to its limits and no matter how hard an athlete might have trained, if he is apathetic towards victory he is not going to make the best use of the physical qualities that his training has developed. The sportsman, sportswoman or athlete who wants to be a champion must first find a driving purpose, an inspired reason for winning. There must be *the will to win*, for this is the way to win as we shall see in Chapter 9.

Chapter Nine
The way to win

Good, well-planned and appropriate training such as has been outlined in this book can take you a long way towards being 'tournament tough' – indeed, without it you never will be. But that elusive quality has elements within it that are difficult to achieve, and which as Jonah Barrington writes (*Murder in the Squash Court*, Stanley Paul, 1982), are 'far beyond the ken of the best sports scientists in the world, and beyond the understanding of the best coaches and trainers'. So we must finally focus our attention on the psychological aspects of success.

The psychology of success

Amongst these elements of tournament toughness is one vital ingredient standing way out from all the rest, and which forms part of the make-up of every champion. It is the will to win. 'This will to win, coupled with the right mental and physical preparation, made John McEnroe one of the world's top players in the most lucrative sport, tennis,' said his coach, Carlos Goffi (*Tournament Tough*, Ebury Press, 1984), speaking of McEnroe's driving obsession to win, of the blazing fire burning inside which made this young man into one of the game's greatest players.

Naturally, sportsmen and women want to win, and the competitive instinct is inherent in most people – but few have the ability to pour every ounce of effort into their game and develop the intense will to win that overcomes all difficulties and setbacks. Why cannot we all do this? Why are so many budding champions daunted by defeats, by feelings of being not quite good enough? Could we not take heart from the example of the young ballet student, Bonny Badusek, who at the age of thirteen broke her neck doing gymnastics? She spent six and a half months in a plaster cast and then turned to tennis. Undaunted! Three months out of the hospital, she played in her first tennis tournament and by the time that she was nineteen she had made 100,000 dollars. When the will to win is there the physical handicaps seem to count for nothing. Indeed, it is surprising how many top-class sportsmen and women were told in their early days that their physical make-up was unpromising material for championship performance. Having the will to win however, overcame physical deficiencies. 'Little Mo', the fabulous Maureen Connolly, perhaps has exemplified this for all time. Small and physically immature though she was, she became at seventeen the Grand Slam champion of world lawn tennis. 'If ever a career could be given a caption, mine was "Win! Win! Win!"' she once said.

But although single-mindedness, the determination to win, is something people are born with, it must be improved upon by hard work, discipline and persistence, whatever the sport. As golfer Gary Player – another Grand Slam champion – was to write in *Gary Player, World Golfer* (F. Thatcher and G. Player, Pelham Books, 1975): 'The person who doesn't work hard, who gives up easily and quits, will never become a winner. A bulldog tenacity is absolutely essential to success in any venture.' It is interesting to note that Gary himself was once told that his small stature and weak musculature would prove a serious disadvantage.

The tenacity and mental power that can drive the body to greater feats can be developed; indeed, it has to be developed by those wishing to reach the top. Motivation, though, must come first. Unless athletes or games players experience a strong drive to succeed they will never put in the effort nor give the attention to detail to perform to maximum capacity. This motivation can be a curious combination of factors. Some people have an inner compulsion to fight hard for success, stemming from a desire for fame or fortune or from the excitement of pitting themselves against risks, overcoming fear, escaping from danger – as with the climber, the lone long-distance sailor and the skier. Today there are rewards enough that are surely motivating – particularly the financial ones. With motivation comes the will to win. Once this is established then the determination to harness the power of the mind inevitably follows. It is this power that can tip the balance one way or another in an even match.

Whether your goal is to win the club championship, the national or the world championship, there is much that can be learnt from studying how the champions themselves found the way to win. It comes down to attitude and attention to detail.

Mental attitude

'A good cricketer is aggressive. By that I don't mean that he is unpleasant, or a cheat or that he argues with umpires or opponents. I mean that he aims to put the opposition under unbearable pressure all the time,' writes Ian Botham (*Cricket*, Cassell, 1980). It is an attitude which pervades the winning strategy of the world's top players. 'You play shots for the positive purpose of upsetting an opponent, mentally, irritating him,' says Jonah Barrington in *Murder in the Squash Court*. It is an approach which we all have to watch out for; we have to keep cool under pressure, for competition at the top becomes a psychological as well as a physical battle. You have to act with the aplomb of an Oscar winner so as to show no sign of nerves or lack of confidence. When things have been going badly, shots not coming off, your drives landing in the rough, and you are well behind with your score, you have to draw upon mental reserves to accept the situation not as a calamity but as a challenge. By keeping cool, controlling your emotions under stress, you can convert an almost disastrous position into an asset. It is the mark of a champion.

It is here that positive thinking comes in. 'The way we think determines what we are and what we can be!' wrote Dr Norman Peale, the New York minister who believed in setting goals and visualising positive results (*The Power of Positive Thinking*, Cedar Books, 1972). It is something borne out by the experience of winners in all walks of life – that if you want something and go for it determinedly you will be astonished at what you can achieve.

It seems that what we have to do is to concentrate on what we are immediately trying to achieve and visualise the successful way to do it. The hurdler before the big race visualises his first accelerating steps to the first hurdle, the high jumper his soaring leap and back arching twist over the bar. They are practising what sports psychologists call 'mental rehearsal', deliberately imagining themselves facing situations and triumphing. Thus they are mentally programmed for success, buoyed up by confidence.

Confidence

The man who always exuded supreme confidence more than anyone else in this century was probably the world heavyweight champion, Mohammed Ali. His oft-repeated words, 'I am the greatest', were no idle boast. He committed himself in public as to how he was going to defeat his next opponent, establishing a psychological advantage, for he usually went into the ring and did just that. His confidence was based on thorough preparation – mental and physical. He paced himself through all his fights, watching for weaknesses, patiently biding his time until the right moment came, then, confident that he had the power and stamina to see him through, he would suddenly go into the attack and 'sting like a bee'.

A player's confidence, though, is constantly under attack, whatever the sport; even in what used to be the gentlemanly game of cricket. England batsman, Andrew Lloyd, recalls being knocked out by a 'bouncer', spending five days in hospital and on his return to the crease hearing the wicket-keeper and slip fielders imploring the fast bowler to 'let him have it'. As Lloyd was later to say: 'A bouncer is not aimed at a batsman's body, it is aimed at his spirit. Cricket is hard. The ball is hard – it hurts. It takes a special sort of person to be good at it. It is not just a physical matter. Facing a bouncer demands mental courage because the bouncer is a mental problem. A good bouncer unsettles you and it makes you play the next good-length ball to the wicket-keeper because you are hesitant in your mind. Doubts get the batsman out; *confidence makes all the difference.* You play your strokes better.'

So many sportsmen now subscribe to this belief. Consequently the acquisition of confidence and control of this mental strength is becoming the increasing concern of the sports psychologist. His trade is an expanding one. For example, there is a course for 'sports enhancement' run in Portland, Oregon, which helps those who have lost their confidence and are finding, because of this, that their game is severely affected. British and United States Open Golf champion Johnny

Miller was so worried about his own loss of confidence that he invested £6,000 on a week-long course run by psychologist Chuck Hogan. 'The course was all about imagery, visualisation and positive thinking,' said Miller (*Daily Telegraph*, 2 August 1985), 'You learn to banish all negative thoughts and tell yourself – "This shot is a piece of cake", then you walk up and hit it like a real champion.' Again it boils down to confidence.

The wizard of the dribble, Argentina's Diego Maradona, once explained to a reporter that to beat an opponent with the ball you had to be supremely confident and have such a sense of superiority that it created a corresponding feeling of inferiority, of failure and frustration, in your opponents so that they became excessively anxious, hesitant and consequently made mistakes.

The effect of a positive mental approach can often be seen in a football match when ten men have fought with so much spirit, spurred on by the crowd's roar, that instead of being severely handicapped they have risen above themselves and played better than when all eleven were fit and on the field. Here again we have a forceful demonstration of the power of the mind to drive the body on to extraordinary efforts. They believe that they can win, and so, often against the odds, they do.

Sometimes, then, it is the crowd that lifts men and women to match-winning form; sometimes it is the individual who motivates himself by psychological insight; and sometimes it is the craft of the coach. This contribution should never be overlooked.

The coach

Few athletes, sportsmen or women reach the top alone; most have been brought on by good coaching and helped along the way by many other enthusiastic, unpaid and unsung heroes. *En route* to the top the best will experience moments of near despair and frustration. There will be times when one injury seems to follow quickly upon another and the situation can be made worse by other unforeseeable setbacks. It is at these times that talking problems through can bring new hope and bolster determination to overcome difficulties.

'I need someone out there to watch my moods,' says top golfer Lee Trevino (*Observer*, 21 July 1985), 'someone to pump me up or settle me down.' Everyone has this need, especially those at the top where the pressures are great and there is everything to lose.

An experienced, knowledgeable coach is a treasure; he can separate himself from the excitement enough to assess conditions and make calm logical decisions. He can take pressure off his protégé and put it upon opponents. In time an uncanny relationship develops so that he understands the men and women under his care; he knows what makes them tick and can instil in them the desire to do everything possible – and more – to win. In fact, one of the most important aspects of a coach's job is to guide the player or athlete into a programme of carefully graded competition, with few easy wins and where he has to fight all the way. There is a lot to be learnt from playing in a class above one's immediate ability, but there is also the danger of losing heart by being consistently beaten. The player who has to battle through to the finals of his class gains experience of playing matches where 'centre court nerves' are vital to success. Eventually skill becomes so conditioned that the movements are performed in a consistent pattern.

The coach can do much in this respect. Look at it this way. There is as much difference between serving an ace in a Sunday afternoon knock-up and serving one at match-point in a critical game as there is between walking calmly along the pavement and walking along a metal platform 300 metres up the Eiffel Tower. The movements are the same but the situation is different. Pavement walking is no training for high girder stunts and tennis practice is of limited value without the stress of fierce competition. And this is where the good coach comes into his own. Finding a good one can save a player valuable time and energy. Nevertheless, no-one should feel entirely dependent upon one.

Equipment

Shortly before golf champion Sandy Lyle was due to take part in the £80,000 Glasgow Open at Haggs Castle in August 1985, his favourite golf clubs were stolen. One of these clubs, his driver, had been specially made for him. Nevertheless with borrowed clubs he completed a creditable round.

In the final of the 4 × 400 metres relay in the 1986 European Athletic Championships at Stuttgart, Britain's third runner, Brian Whittle, had his shoe ripped off his foot during the handover. He never wavered or flinched but ran on so well, with one shoe off and one shoe on, that Britain won the race in a magnificent time of 2 minutes 59.85 seconds. It was a race which will live in everyone's memory for years to come not only for the 'seven shoe' victory but also for the fact that hours before the race, two of the four team members dropped out through sickness. Two substitutes went in and one later said, 'We ran on anger, determined to win despite the setbacks.'

The moral of stories such as these is surely that although having the right equipment is very important it is still not the be-all and end-all as long as no-one gets upset. In these instances, calamity was turned into a motivating challenge. But it doesn't always work out that way. Having equipment that suits you best can make all the difference between winning and being an also-ran.

However, equipment today is becoming more and more sophisticated. New synthetic materials give firms the opportunity of making equipment lighter or heavier, larger or smaller, to cater for players of every size and shape, from age eight to eighty. The range of gear is so extensive that the ordinary club player is often left bewildered as to choice. It is worth paying close attention to these new developments, though, and seeking specialist guidance. Time and money spent in choosing the right equipment is well spent. Then, having made your choice and paid your money, make sure that you look after it well.

Yes, equipment is important, but do remember also – as we have seen earlier in this chapter – that ultimately you, and not the equipment, are the most important. You must be well prepared for that big day.

Preparation for the big match

'It's panic stations sometimes,' said champion World Miler, Steve Cram, talking about the last few minutes before a big race, 'especially when you know your last time wasn't a big success. You've planned it all out the night before but when you get out there on your own, doubts begin to creep in. "Maybe I shouldn't do that?" you find yourself saying. And it's then that you have to be firm. Concentrate on what you are doing, keep to your planned routine.' Having a routine is really essential and it should be a routine that covers the whole day from the moment you wake. If your pre-match routine is right and total preparation good, then you should be in the best possible mental condition for making the most of your skill and physical ability.

Sebastian Coe, twice Olympic Gold Medallist at 1500 metres, tries to relax knowing that he has done all that he can do to reach peak mental and physical condition for the really big event. He believes that 'It's not possible in the course of an athletic season to peak twice.' For some sportsmen, however, keeping to a peak of performance for months on end is essential. Tennis players, for example, are under tremendous pressure. Consequently their immediate pre-match preparation is worked out in great detail. On tournament days they follow a carefully planned schedule that allows adequate time for everything that has to be done without rushing. John McEnroe, for example, always goes into the changing room a good forty minutes before the time set for the match. There he will stretch his joints and muscles before dressing. His last meal will have been taken three hours earlier and before that he will have loosened up with court practice for about an hour. Thus, his Big Match Day would be structured something like this:

7.15	Rise
7.45	Begin breakfast
8.15	Finish breakfast
9.45	On court for practice
10.45	Finish practice session
11.30	Begin to eat
12.00	Finish meal
14.15	Enter changing room
15.00	Tournament match

What athletes and sportsmen and women have found to be a big help on tournament days is the calming effect of going through a well-known ritual, undressing, putting on kit, limb-shaking and stretching and generally getting mentally prepared. The worst thing to do is to leave insufficient time for the routine so that you have to rush and become anxious instead of going on to the pitch or court calmly and confident that you have now done everything possible to get yourself fit and ready for the match. Now you can really concentrate on gamesmanship and tactics – on the single act of winning. And it is for this moment that all the training – with weights and without – will have been worth while.

Exercises

muscle	exercises
Quadriceps	foot press, leg lifts, squat thrusts, lunges
Hamstrings	knee press, foot on table, leg extensions
Thighs	inner/outer thighs, side leg lifts
Calf	wall push ups, jumps
Abdominal	sit ups, hip thrusts
Back	flying exercise, hip rolls, squats, trunk raising/bending
Shoulder	shrugs
Arms	press up, circles
Adductors	butterfly, squats, inner thigh stretch, inner thigh lift, hip adduct
Achillies tendon	squats

Circuits

exercise	purpose
Treadmills	legs
Pull Ups	arms, shoulder flexors
Squats Thrusts	legs (general endurance)
Press Ups	arms, chest extensors
Sit Ups	abdominal
Step Ups	legs (general endurance)
Trunk Raising	dorsal
Chinnies	abdominal
High knee Runs	legs, arms
Burpees	legs (general endurance)
Bench Jumps	legs
Squat Jumps	legs (general endurance)